10-MINUTE

TIDY HOME

10-MINUTE

TIDY HOME

Hundreds of Easy Tips to Straighten and
Clean Every Room of Your House

WRITTEN BY

SARA L. HUNTER

FAIR WINDS

Inspiring | Educating | Creating | Entertaining

Brimming with creative inspiration, how-to projects, and useful information to enrich your everyday life, Quarto Knows is a favorite destination for those pursuing their interests and passions. Visit our site and dig deeper with our books into your area of interest: Quarto Creates, Quarto Cooks, Quarto Homes, Quarto Lives, Quarto Drives, Quarto Explores, Quarto Gifts, or Quarto Kids.

© 2005, 2019 Quarto Publishing Group USA Inc.

First Published in 2005 by Fair Winds Press, an imprint of The Quarto Group, 100 Cummings Center, Suite 265-D, Beverly, MA 01915, USA. T (978) 282-9590 F (978) 283-2742 QuartoKnows.com

Fair Winds Press titles are also available at discount for retail, wholesale, promotional, and bulk purchase. For details, contact the Special Sales Manager by email at specialsales@quarto.com or by mail at The Quarto Group, Attn: Special Sales Manager, 100 Cummings Center, Suite 265-D, Beverly, MA 01915, USA.

23 22 21 20 19   2 3 4 5

ISBN: 978-1-59233-913-6

Digital edition published in 2019
eISBN: 978-1-63159-815-9

Much of the information within this book was previously published under the title *10-Minute Organizing* by Sara Lavieri Hunter (Fair Winds Press, 2005)

Library of Congress Cataloging-in-Publication Data available under *10-Minute Organizing*.

Design and Illustration: Tanya Jacobson, crsld.co

Printed in China

I DEDICATE THIS BOOK TO MY SISTER, HOLLY.

Holly was there to poke fun at my need for clean in the beginning. She was there to try to bring me back when my tendencies became borderline obsessive-compulsive. Most importantly, she was there to tell me I needed to write this book because there are people who can benefit from my insanity.

Contents

Getting Started   8

PART ONE: All Around the House

1 In the Kitchen   14
2 Bathroom Break   32
3 Living Room Roundup   44
4 Playroom Psychology   50
5 Bedrooms: Yours   56
6 Bedrooms: Theirs   64
7 Making the Home Office Work   76
8 Laundry Room Logic   96
9 Storage Solutions   102
10 The Garbage-Free Garage   110

PART TWO: Entertaining

11 Havoc-less Holidays   118
12 Houseguests Welcome   134
13 Parties: Yours   142
14 Parties: Theirs   154

PART THREE: On the Move

15 Vacations and Business Trips   170
16 Making Your Move   192

About the Author   206
Index   207

Getting Started

Organization was not always so easy for me. My mother will tell you that when I was a teenager, my bedroom was a pigsty! Things such as dirty clothes, records, books, and shoes piled up, and when I finally put my mind to it, it took me hours to clean my room. I'll even go so far to admit that it was nearly impossible to dust because of all the clutter! Going out with friends, talking for hours on the telephone, and dancing to blaring music seemed much more important.

I grew up, moved out, and to my mother's surprise, I learned how to keep a tidy house. With each move, I became a little neater and a little more organized. My first apartment was a little neater than my bedroom at home, my second apartment was neater than the first, and my first house was so well organized that family members began to question my sanity. Once I moved into my second house, I began to question my sanity!

WHY ORGANIZE?

There are many benefits to leading an organized life, but perhaps most important is that it tends to rub off on the people around you, including your significant other and children. (Do I have your attention now?)

Put the phrase "you can't teach an old dog new tricks" to rest, and encourage your spouse to clean the mail off the counter, put his shoes away, and stop throwing dirty laundry on the floor. Does he think the dirty clothes pick themselves up off the floor and jump into the hamper? I think not.

Fortunately, children are like sponges, and they're ready to absorb good habits and clean tendencies. Think of it this way: If you start teaching your children to organize their lives now, you'll not only simplify your life but also raise organized adults and helpful spouses.

Remember, good deeds come back full circle! This particular deed will come back to you twofold. First, your children will be more independent and won't rely on you to do their laundry and pick up after them. Second, your children's future spouses will be grateful to you for teaching their husband or wife good habits, and thus, they'll be indebted to you. (At least, that's what I'm hoping for!)

ORGANIZING GETS EASIER

Luckily, organizing is one of those things that get easier with time. It's like exercise: Once you start, you'll never want to stop, and there's no time like the present to start!

If you put some thought and effort into it, you can organize anything. There is a way to organize every room in your house and every aspect of your life, from party planning to travel. If you've never really thought about getting yourself organized, start off slowly with a few simple tasks. For example, spend a few minutes organizing the magazines in your living room, or getting rid of old makeup and expired medications. Once you get the hang of it, move on to the rest of your house!

No matter what, always take it a little at a time. Plunging in full-tilt and working for hours is the surest road to giving up. That's why I've made sure the tips in this book take only ten minutes (or less) to do, so you'll never feel overwhelmed. You'll be amazed at what you can do in just ten minutes!

One final thought before we begin: Remember that organization is good for your well-being, so take control of your life *and* your living room. Everything has a place, and it's up to you to find it!

PART ONE

All Around the House

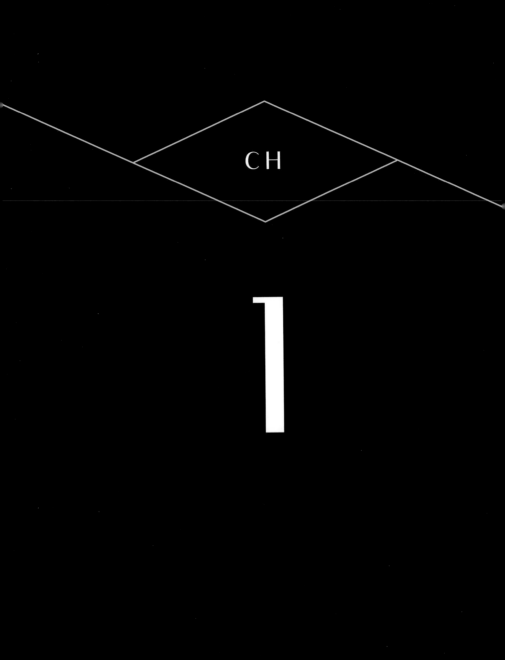

CH

1

IN THE KITCHEN

The kitchen may be the heart of the home, but it's often the heart of a family's chaos. So let's start our organizing efforts here. Remember, an organized kitchen is an efficient kitchen. Even if you're not much of a cook, you will work better when you know where to find things.

Clean out your flatware drawer and put utensils in a tray.

Flatware trays come in a variety of styles and sizes, and they are great for organizing your utensils. Empty your drawer of its jumble of tangled implements, and wash both the drawer and the utensils. Then set a tray into the drawer, and place the utensils in their proper place. If your drawer is large enough, you can buy a tray with space for serving utensils as well.

Store cooking utensils in a crock.

Remove cooking implements from the flatware drawer and store them in a nice crock on the stovetop. Regardless of how your kitchen is set up, it doesn't make sense to run back and forth for cooking utensils. Put all of your spatulas, whisks, tongs, ladles, and cooking spoons in a convenient crock on top of or next to the stove.

Store all stainless steel bowls and covers inside one another.

Stainless steel bowls are meant to fit inside one another. Instead of resting them all on a shelf, put them inside one another in order of size.

Place all pans on top of each other.

Using vertical space allows you to fit more into your cabinets. Stack your pans with the biggest one on the bottom. Make sure the handles are facing out so you can easily grab them.

Store all pots inside of one another.

As long as you're organizing your cookware cabinet, stack your pots the same way, too.

Use pullout shelves to house lids.

Mount a pullout shelf to house the lids for your pots and pans. If you do this in the same cabinet as your pots and pans, you won't have to waste time searching for a pan with a matching lid.

Organize cookbooks alphabetically, or by topic.

It's easy to get inundated with best-selling cookbooks, so make sure you organize them on a shelf *as you purchase them*. Use a system—alphabetical, by author, or by topic—that works for you.

Put all recipes in a small storage box.

People of all cooking capabilities have recipes from blogs, family members, and friends. Organize your hard copy recipes in a box so they won't get misplaced—you can even use dividers to separate your recipes by topic. Or, you can scan your recipes and file them along with any that you've found online in a folder on your computer desktop or in the cloud. If you're big into bookmarking online recipes, create a folder within the bookmarks bar and store all of your favorite links there.

Store magazine recipes or other large pages in clear sheet protectors.
I love clipping recipes from magazines such as *Cooking Light* and *Bon Appetit*,
but the full-page recipes won't fit into my recipe box unless I fold them
twice. I *need* those recipes because I'm a person who needs a picture to cook
by, but not the aggravation of unfolding the recipes like a paper puzzle
every time I need it! Luckily, I've discovered a way to manage them. If you
store these recipes in clear plastic folders and file them into a binder, you
won't be left wondering, "Is this what it's supposed to look like?"

Store fruit on a two-tiered tray or basket.
The more counter space you have, the more organized you will be! Put
your fruit in a two-tiered tray or basket to take advantage of vertical space,
and save room on the counter. Make sure that everyone in your family can
reach it.

Put all spice jars on a carousel.
Time is of the essence when adding spices to your recipes. Instead of
keeping spices on cabinet shelves, organize them on a carousel so they can
be easily found in a pinch.

Store seasoning packets in a recipe box.
Seasoning packets are a great way to add flavor to many foods, but
storing them can be a challenge. They often get crumpled and torn when
they're thrown into a cabinet, leaving you with a powdery mess to clean
up. From now on, keep your seasoning packets in a recipe box. You can
even alphabetize them, or organize them according to flavor to make
cooking easier!

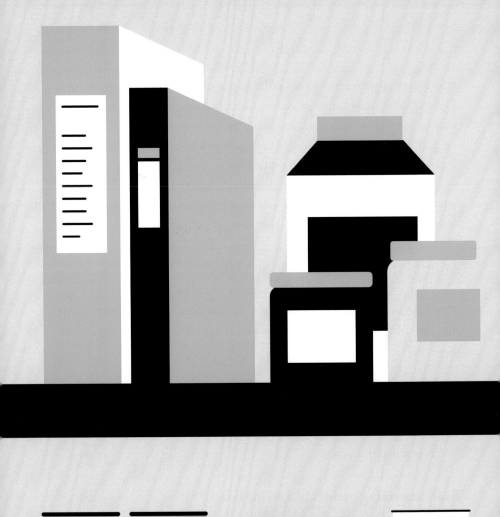

Arrange canned goods alphabetically.

Just kidding—I'm not that crazy! You don't need to go so far as to alphabetize your canned goods, but they should be organized. How many times have you bought soup at the store, only to discover that you have five cans of it in the back of your cabinet? If you stack your soups and other canned goods facing out, with same kinds on top of one another, you'll always know what you have on hand.

Put cereal in sealed containers with pouring spouts.

If you're short on cabinet space, it can be challenging to store multiple boxes of cereal. I know that mine always end up on top of the fridge! If you put your cereal inside sealed containers, they'll look nicer on your counter, can be poured into a bowl more easily, will remain bug-free, and stay fresh longer.

Organize your snack cupboard into family member favorites.

Everyone has their favorite snack, and it's hard enough to get going in the morning without digging through the cabinet for your child's favorite munchies. Organize your snack cupboard into sections for each family member: one for you, one for your partner, and one for your child. It's easy to pack food for the day when it's in one location. Another timesaver: Show your family members where their snacks are and let them pack their own!

Install hooks to hang frequently used mugs near the coffee pot.
We have so many mugs in our house that it can be hazardous to try to remove a favorite one from the pile. Install a few cup hooks on the wall near your coffee maker, and hang your favorite mugs for everyone to see and use. That way, you've organized your coffee station and saved space in your cabinets.

Store all tea bags together in one canister.
In our house, everyone likes different types of tea. Instead of cramming four boxes of tea into the cabinet, I remove the tea bags from the boxes and put them in a decorative canister on my counter top. Not only do I save space, I save time when making a cup of tea.

Store your baking pans under the oven.
Baking pans and cookie sheets come in a variety of different sizes and can take up a lot of space. Most people wouldn't think of putting glasses or dinner plates in the oven drawer, but it's a perfect place for your baking pans and cookie sheets. They'll be in a drawer so they won't get dusty, and they'll be in a central location.

Hang your pots and pans.
If cabinet space is an issue for you, mount several heavy-duty hooks on your ceiling from which to hang your pots and pans. Think vertically!

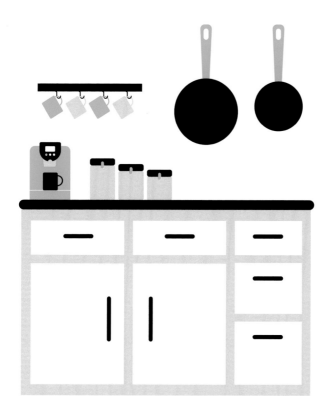

Put all unused kitchen appliances in a pantry cabinet.

We all have kitchen appliances that we haven't actually used in a year, so why should we keep them on our counter tops? If you don't regularly use an appliance, put it in your pantry to save space.

Organize your glasses and cups by height.

Stack tall glasses on one shelf, shorter juice glasses on another shelf, and mugs on the third shelf. Determine which shelves will be used for what based on how often you use a particular type of glass or mug.

Organize your plates by size.

Keep your lunch plates stacked separately from your dinner plates, so that you don't have to move them as often, and they won't chip as easily. Organize vegetable bowls and serving platters in their own cabinet.

If you keep serving bowls and platters with your plates, you're asking for trouble! I have broken so many plates and serving bowls trying to balance them on top of one another. Store your serving pieces in a separate cabinet so they're easily accessible.

Get each family member their own reusable water bottle.

Go green, save space, and stay organized all at the same time by getting a unique reusable water bottle for everyone in your household. The days of single-use plastic water bottles are waning, but staying hydrated can still be easy. With everyone assigned a certain bottle, there will be no confusion and no waste—just grab your bottle, fill it, and go!

Put your plastic wrap, aluminum foil, wax paper, and storage bags in one drawer.

Most experts say to wrap and put away leftover food while it's hot, instead of letting it sit out on your counter. If you store all of your aluminum foil, plastic wrap, wax paper, and storage bags in a drawer near your fridge or counter, you can quickly take care of your leftovers without breaking any rules.

Store all plastic storage containers inside one another.

Most Tupperware cabinets are impossible to open without being attacked by toppling containers! To avoid similar disaster and save space, store all plastic storage containers inside one another and organize them according to size.

Throw away old food from the fridge.

This may sound obvious, but listen up: Clean your refrigerator on a regular basis! I organize my fridge and wipe it clean every week before I go grocery shopping. It's nearly empty at that point, so it's quick and easy to wipe down the shelves. Once your fridge is clean, organize your food into groups. For example, I have all of our beverages on one shelf; meat, cheese, yogurt, and eggs on another; and snack foods and leftovers on the bottom shelf. If you make an effort to do this each week, you'll find it easy to keep your fridge organized and clean.

Throw away freezer-burned food.

There is no sense in keeping freezer-burned food that no one is ever going to eat, so make an effort to regularly clean your freezer, and throw out the undesirables!

Take juice boxes out of plastic wrap so they're easily accessible.

Items tend to be over-packaged these days, thus taking up more room in your refrigerator. Remove juice boxes from their packaging before stacking them in your fridge. Not only will you save space but also your kids can easily grab the boxes themselves, without your assistance.

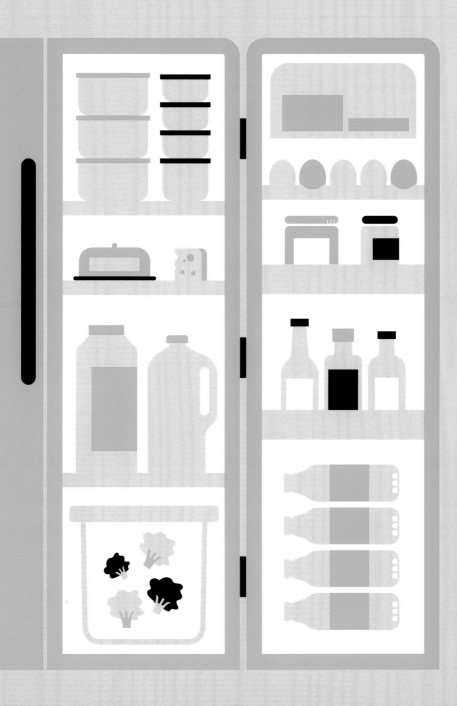

Keep cleaners and sponges in a tote under the sink.

The cabinet under the kitchen sink is home to everything from cleaners to vases, and it's important to keep things in their place. You don't want to topple your vases while reaching for a slimy sponge! Instead, store kitchen cleaning supplies and sponges in a clear tote. Not only will they be easy to grab, they'll be clean when you're ready to use them.

Clean out dishtowels and discard old ones.

Dishtowels should be frequently washed and replaced. They are not meant to last a lifetime! However, people rarely get rid of them. Take five minutes to sort through your pile of dishtowels and get rid of the ones with holes. Then make two piles of the remaining towels. The first pile is for older, faded towels that can be used for baking and drying dishes. The second pile of newer towels can be hung on your stove handle for wet hands. Did you know that the wrinkles come out of a dishtowel after you use it to dry your hands a few times?

Put your potholders on top of the fridge.

Instead of hanging potholders from your oven or stove, put them in a nice basket on top of your fridge, or in a corner of the counter with your dishtowels. When you organize like items together, you will always know where to find them in a pinch.

Sort through your coupon holder or try going digital.
If you still clip coupons from newspapers, it is worth it to invest in a
coupon holder because they come with different sections for everything
you'd ever want to buy. Just make sure you sort through the coupons every
month and toss the ones that have expired. Be sure to check for digital
coupons or coupon codes as well, which you can organize on your phone
or through various smartphone apps. Not only will this save you space
in your kitchen, but it will also mean much less fumbling through your
wallet at the cash register.

**Keep pens and paper in a picture-frame caddy on a kitchen
island or counter.**
This is a great way to frame a cute picture *and* keep all of your writing utensils
and paper in one neat place. Much more efficient than the junk drawer!

Use a small plastic binder to store all pertinent family information.
A family binder is a great way to keep contact information organized. Store
items such as phone numbers, take-out menus, and work schedules in a
binder, divided into organized sections, and keep this binder near your
house phone or in a drawer.

Use a hanging basket to store your mail and bills.
Despite the prevalence of online bill paying systems, many people still
like to get hard copies in the mail. To keep all of those papers organized—
which will also help to make sure the bills get paid on time—put all of your
mail in a nice basket hanging by the stairs or in your home office. It makes
life easier to just grab the basket and have everything in one place when it's
time to take care of the bills that we don't pay automatically or online.

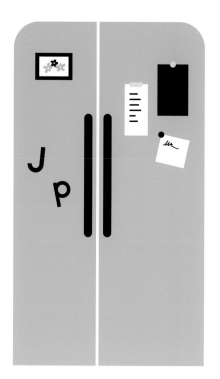

Hang a magnetic pad on the fridge to use for shopping lists.

It's hard for me to believe that some people actually go grocery shopping without a list! I constantly need to make lists. It's not that I'll actually forget something, just that I think I will! Thankfully, my wonderful husband started stuffing magnetic shopping lists into my Christmas stocking each year in order to eliminate the rows of sticky notes on our kitchen island.

Use magnetic clips to hang kids' artwork on the fridge.
Once kids start school, they bring home beautiful artwork every day. After you *ooh* and *aah* over it, hang it on the fridge with a magnetic clip. That way, your fridge isn't completely covered with taped-on pieces of artwork, and you can easily change them with new ones.

Arrange pictures in a magnetic frame on the fridge.
Instead of mounting your pictures with magnets, use decorative magnetic frames. It looks much nicer, and actually makes the front of your fridge look somewhat organized!

Use a magnetic photo frame to store take-out menus.
Unlike my younger sister, I think of cooking as a chore, so I am always ready to pack it in and order take-out. We have at least twenty take-out menus, and I keep them tucked away in a magnetic photo frame on the side of my fridge. This way, they are contained, and everyone knows where to find them.

Use a magnetic white board to jot down contact information.
If you hire a babysitter every now and then, you must have all your contact information in a visible place. Hang a white board on the wall near your house phone or on your refrigerator, and write down your cell phone numbers, the children's doctor's name and telephone number, and the name and number of a friend, relative, or neighbor to contact in case of emergency.

CH

2

BATHROOM
BREAK

B elieve it or not, organizing a bathroom is easy—and you'll be so glad you did it! The key is to stay on top of things, and not fall back into your old habit of just shoving things under the sink. Use these tips to keep your bathroom neat and organized—you'll never waste time looking for things, or buying another replacement you don't really need.

Throw away all dried-out toiletries.
If you don't use it, lose it. It's tempting to take freebies home from the mall or to hang on to lotions and soaps because you received them as gifts, but don't! You'll be amazed by how much space you gain in your bathroom by getting rid of old toiletries.

Fill a travel bag with extra toiletries so you're ready to go.
It's inevitable that you'll leave for a vacation and forget your deodorant. Prepare ahead of time by throwing a few cotton squares, swabs, liners, a little tube of toothpaste, a new toothbrush, travel-size shampoo and conditioner, and a stick of deodorant into your travel bag. Your toiletries will be ready to go when you are! When you return from a trip, replenish the items so you're ready for the next one.

Use a drawer organizer to store cosmetics.
Cosmetics such as eyeshadow palettes and pressed powders become cracked and break into pieces when they are constantly shuffled around. Use a drawer to keep your cosmetics intact and in order.

Discard old makeup that hasn't been used in months.

I know, that flaming red lipstick looked great on you when you were in college—and it's difficult to throw away makeup before you finish it. But trust me, makeup *does* expire, and its packaging indicates how long it is safe to use after being opened. Toss it if the date has passed or if you used it when you had an infection. For example, throw out eye makeup you wore when you had pink eye.

Store nail polish in a basket so it's easily accessible.

Summer means flip flops, and flip flops mean neat feet! Put all of your pedicure materials—polish, remover, cotton balls or squares, files, and so on—in a little basket that can be grabbed quickly for emergency touch-ups.

Store styling tools in a storage bag so they don't get lost or dirty.

When you're getting all dolled up, the last thing you need is dust bunnies in your hair! Keep your curling irons and flat irons in duster bags and your hot rollers in their carrying cases so everything stays nice and clean—including your luscious locks!

Throw away all expired medications.

Have you ever had a pounding headache and gone into the medicine cabinet for some relief, only to find that all your ibuprofen has expired? I have, and it's not amusing. Medications lose effectiveness once they expire, so check their dates every once in a while and replace them as needed.

Keep children's medications separate from adult medications.

When your child is up in the middle of the night with a fever, you don't want to grab the wrong medication in a sleepy haze. To be safe, put all adult medications in one section of the cabinet or drawer and your children's in another. And of course, keep all medications out of reach of tiny hands!

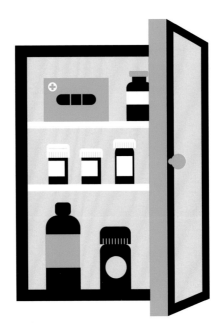

Keep dosage amounts on a paper tucked inside each box of medicine.
If your child is under six years old, the dosage directions on most
medications will tell you to call your doctor. If your child has a low-grade
fever or some other minor ailment, you don't want to have to track down
the doctor. Next time your doctor gives you a dosage, write down the date,
weight, and age of your child, in addition to the exact dosage amount. Next
time, you won't have to call!

Store cotton swabs in a jar.
Cotton swab boxes take up precious space in a crowded medicine cabinet.
To conserve space, store the box underneath the sink, and put a handful of
swabs in a jar in the cabinet or in a decorative container on the counter.

Store cotton squares or balls in a jar or basket.
Cotton squares (and balls) are extremely useful! They can be used to apply
toner to your face, touch up nail polish, clean earrings, and so on. Keep
them in a little basket so they're never out of reach.

Hang tweezers, nail clippers, and scissors inside the cabinet door.
Scissors become dull when they're thrown into a cabinet with a million
other things. To keep scissors, tweezers, and nail clippers sharp, hang them
inside the cabinet. Just be sure to lock it if little hands can reach the door!

Install one towel hook for each family member.

Towels, especially if they're thick and absorbent, need a place to dry. It takes seconds to mount a towel hook, and you can choose from many different styles to fit your decor. If your children have their own hooks, it will encourage them to hang up their towels rather than toss them on the floor. The same goes for bathrobes.

Install a towel bar specifically for a face and hand towel.

Hooks are great for bath towels, but you really need a towel bar for your washcloth and hand towel. They'll dry faster when spread out on a towel bar.

Arrange towels by size.

Don't just throw your towels into a linen closet, where people have to paw through the whole pile to find the one they want. Instead, stack your towels according to size, so that bath towels are in one pile, hand towels in another, and washcloths in yet another. It will help you *and* your guests!

Remove bar soaps from plastic wrap and store them with your towels.
According to my Dad, I have the best-smelling towels. I'm not sure if it's because of the two dryer sheets, or if it's because I unwrap my bar soaps and sit them on the shelf with the towels. The aroma fills the linen closet, making everything smell fresh and clean. If you unwrap the soaps before you put them away, you'll not only freshen up your linen closet, you'll save yourself time. It's much easier to just grab a bar before hopping in the shower instead of struggling with the plastic wrap.

Organize guest towels in a decorative basket with scented soaps or candles.
Before you fold guest towels and place them in a basket, put some unwrapped votive candles or scented soaps in the bottom of the basket to make the towels smell nice. (Just don't use colored candles or soaps that could potentially bleed onto the towels!)

Store seasonal items in the back of the linen closet.
Keep all of the things you don't use regularly, such as a Christmas soap dispenser, in the back of the linen closet. Keep like items together so they're easy to find when it's time to use them.

Store magazines and books in a magazine rack or basket.

I used to clean a friend's house, and he kept his bathroom reading material on the back of the toilet. Just a few weeks after I started cleaning for him, I had my first mishap. After I cleaned the toilet, I put his magazines back on the tank cover while it was still wet. Not a smart thing to do! The magazines stuck to the toilet, and the paper bits never did come off completely. The moral of this story: Store your bathroom reading materials in a nice basket or rack on the floor near the toilet. They'll be much easier to grab when needed and won't make a mess.

Keep toothbrushes organized in a cup or toothbrush holder.

My family will tell you that I'm a little obsessed with germs. I don't understand how someone can leave his toothbrush—something that is used to clean the inside of his mouth—on a dirty bathroom counter. The very thought makes me cringe! That said, please keep your toothbrush in a cup or in a toothbrush holder with separate sections. Make sure each family member's toothbrush is a different color to avoid spreading germs.

Hang decorative shelves for frequently used items.

Keeping all of your daily cleaners and styling products handy can be challenging, especially if you don't have a sizeable vanity top. Use wrought-iron shelves to keep hair gels, sprays, and the like off the counter but in easy reach.

Organize all cleaning supplies and toxic items under the sink with a cabinet lock.

You'll save a lot of time if you keep your cleaning supplies in the area to be cleaned. If you have small children, make sure you have a lock on the cabinet door.

Organize extra supplies into groups.

If you're a fan of the wholesale clubs, you're no stranger to storing duplicates of frequently used products. To make your life easier, organize surplus supplies into groups in the bathroom cabinet. For example, keep shampoos and conditioners together, facial cleaners and lotions together, and so on and so forth.

Hang razors on the shower wall.

It's important to keep razors away from little hands! I always tried to fit my razor on the shelf next to my soap, but it constantly fell on the floor. Mount a suctioned hook on your shower wall to keep your razor up and out of the way.

Store all bath toys in a mesh bag inside the shower.

If you have a small bathroom, keep your bath toys in the shower. Buy a mildew-resistant mesh bag and hang it from the showerhead or on the wall with suction cups.

Keep bath cups and large toys in a bucket on the floor.

When my daughter moved into the big tub, I bought her a new bath toy to help her adjust. I didn't realize it then, but the Ernie car was too big for the mesh bag I had hung on the shower wall. What to do? Place a bucket in the corner of the bathroom, next to the tub, and fill it with large bath toys and cups for rinsing hair.

3

LIVING ROOM
ROUNDUP

A living room should be lived in not lived out of. Think of how you feel every time the doorbell rings when you're not expecting company. Is the first thought that runs through your mind, "What if they come in here?" Simplify and consolidate to take care of that anxiety and make your life easier.

Digitize your home videos.

Depending on your age, you or your family may have some home movies on VHS tape. Not only is watching them inconvenient—do you even know where your VCR is?—but storing precious memories on delicate rolls of film is risky, especially if there is only one copy. For easier access and guaranteed preservation, get your home movies digitized. Then you can store DVDs in a safe location or upload those digital files onto a hard drive or cloud storage.

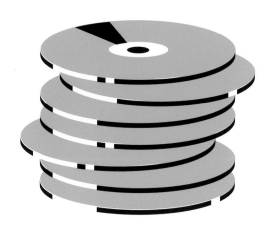

Organize CDs and DVDs.

If you still own discs or simply prefer them to streaming services and digital formats, put in the effort to keep these items organized and scratch-free. Store the discs near their respective playback machines in a tower or nice box and organize them alphabetically or by category. If you collect vinyl, the same rules apply.

Sort through old magazines and discard the ones you're through with.

Does anyone else have unread magazines from last summer? I make a conscious effort to discard magazines that are outdated or uninteresting. If you sort them regularly, it isn't that much of a hassle. If you don't want to discard them, give them to your dentist or doctor to keep in their waiting rooms. Just remember to cut out your address before donating them!

Store magazines in a nice basket.

Everyone has a place to throw their magazines when they arrive, whether it's on the counter, table, or ottoman. Keep your surfaces clear by giving those magazines a home of their own. Place a nice wicker basket in the corner of your living room or near an armchair. If you don't have time to read the magazines when they arrive, simply place them in the basket so they'll be out of sight until you're ready to sit down and read.

Stow candles and candle holders in an end table.

Collect all your votives and tea lights and put them in the drawer of an end table. Not only are they in a central location, but they'll also fill your living room with smells of the season!

Hang jackets and hats on a coat rack.

Keeping a coat rack in your living room will alleviate the need to throw guests' jackets on your bed or to try to squeeze them into a hall closet. People can easily take their own coats when they're ready to leave.

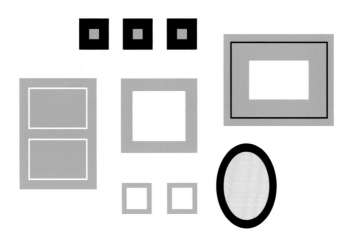

Hang framed family pictures on a staircase wall.

Do you have lots of pictures sitting around your house? My entertainment center had so many photos on it that my dad nicknamed it "the shrine!" It was then that I decided to hang the family pictures on the staircase wall. Not only do I enjoy them more, but guests like to look at them too.

Put all toys and balls in a toy box.

It's very easy for a home to become overrun with toys! My advice: Put all of the toys and balls into a nice toy box that will blend into your room. For example, our toy box matches the wood of our entertainment center and end tables. It doesn't stick out like a sore thumb and makes our living room look much nicer.

Hang a letter rack/key hook by your front door.

When we got married, my husband's Aunt Elsie sent us a wooden key and letter rack. At first I thought, "Why do I need something else to hang on the wall?" But it soon became a necessity! We always know where our keys are and don't have to waste time looking for them.

CH

4

PLAYROOM
PSYCHOLOGY

Okay, I know what you're thinking: How do you organize a playroom? But where there's a will, there's a way! Set it up so that your kids can easily find what they're looking for, and they'll know where to put away toys when they're done.

Store toy cars in a plastic tote.

I'm not sure what the attraction is, but all kids love toy cars. My daughter had a favorite—a red Ferrari that was often misplaced. It's hard to keep track of one car when you have piles of them everywhere! I decided to organize her toy cars once and for all, so I set up a plastic tote in her closet and labeled it for easy reference. When she finished playing with the cars, they went back into the box and we always knew where to find that red Ferrari.

Put all dolls in a plastic tote.

Most little kids have a favorite doll, but how many did you buy before a favorite emerged? If you want to keep all of the dolls—in case your child has a change of heart or has friends over to play—store them in a plastic tote that can be used as a doll bed during pretend play. Don't forget to label it!

Store all art supplies in a clear plastic tote.

Encouraging a budding artist is one of the greatest things a parent can do. Children learn to express themselves through art at a very young age. But art supplies can get messy and take up a lot of space. Store supplies in a labeled plastic tote, so they're easy to find and the mess is contained.

Put all trains and track accessories in a large plastic tote.

Trains are a great way to occupy children of all ages, but it can be difficult to store them if they didn't come in a wooden box. Store all trains, tracks, and accessories in a large plastic tote so they stay together and are easy to drag out. Don't forget to label the tote!

Arrange all plastic totes on a shelf.

After you label plastic totes and fill them with various toys, art supplies, and dolls, you'll need a place to keep them. Put them on the shelves in your kids' closets so they can easily reach them. If your child's closet doesn't have shelves, stack the totes neatly on the floor.

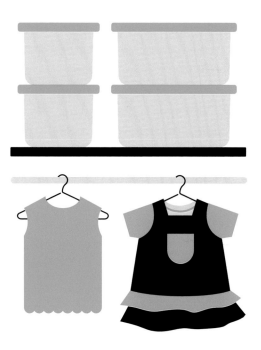

Store building blocks in a large bucket with a cover.
It's hard to build a tower when half the blocks are missing. Keep all building blocks in a covered bucket so they don't get lost around the house.

Arrange small toys on a shelf in storage bins.
If you have kids of different ages or one child who has a variety of different interests, invest in a shelf with plastic storage bins. Organize the playthings by age group or by type. For example, put infant toys in one bin and trucks in another.

Organize doll clothes in a basket or tote.

Keeping track of Barbie shoes and outfits is nearly impossible. The shoes get sucked up in the vacuum, and bits and pieces of the outfits are always vanishing! To avoid future fashion disasters, store all doll clothes in a plastic tote or wicker basket and label it so you and your children know where to find them.

Stack all board games on a bookshelf or game table.

Board games need to be kept organized so that you don't lose any of the pieces. Losing one piece can ruin an entire game! Keep your game pieces in the right box, in a storage bag if necessary, and stack the boxes to save space.

Keep all playhouse dishes and utensils together.

Neaten your child's playhouse the way you neaten *your* house! Stack the dishes and put the utensils in a cup so your child is ready to host when the doorbell rings.

Store all play food in a basket.

Some play food comes in a pretend grocery basket and that's the perfect place to store it when your child isn't cooking something. If your play food didn't come in a basket, you can buy a wicker one at a craft store and use it to keep the plastic fruits and vegetables together.

CH

5

BEDROOMS:
YOURS

S omeone once told me that you should never do anything but sleep in your bedroom, especially if you have difficulty falling asleep. The theory is that if your body is trained to only sleep in the bedroom, it'll know that it's time to sleep when you enter the room. I never tested that theory, but I figure the more organized my bedroom is, the better I'll sleep!

Store socks, lingerie, and pantyhose in one dresser drawer.
You've organized your child's dresser, now organize your own! Keep all of your unmentionables in one drawer. Separate them into piles of panties, bras, slips, pantyhose, and socks.

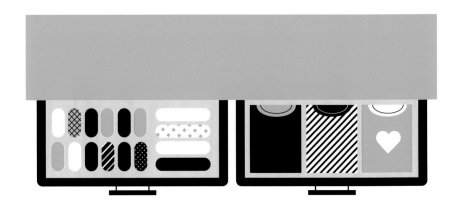

Store shorts and short-sleeved T-shirts in another drawer.

I may move winter clothes from my closet in the spring, but I'm not so ambitious as to tackle my dresser. If you feel the same way, simply organize by season. Keep all of your shorts and short-sleeved T-shirts in a drawer with bathing suits and cover-ups.

Store running pants, sweatpants, and long-sleeved shirts in a third drawer.

Designate a winter drawer and separate it into piles of sweatpants, running pants, and long-sleeved T-shirts.

Store all pajamas in their own drawer.

You can organize pajamas, too! Separate your summer pajamas from your winter pajamas. Getting ready for bed just got easier!

Put dirty clothes in a hamper.

Why is it so hard to lift the cover of a hamper and drop in your dirty clothes? I know it's probably the last thing on your mind each morning when you're rushing out the door, but think of what a nice neat room you'll come home to if you take an extra few seconds to clean up that pile of clothes. Keep a hamper handy, and get in the habit of using it.

Store winter clothes in totes under the bed.

Once winter is over and you don't have to wear three layers to keep warm, store those bulky clothes under the bed. Out of sight, out of mind! Time to make room for spring and summer clothes!

Use robe hooks to hang robes behind the door.

I'm one of those people who would like her house to look like it jumped out of *Better Homes & Gardens* magazine, so I can't stand having things out of place. As easy as it is to throw a robe on the footboard of the bed, it's just as easy to hang it on a hook behind your bedroom door. And it's so much neater!

Keep magazines and books in the bottom of your nightstand.

A nightstand has two purposes. One is to display things such as pictures, an alarm clock, and a lamp. The other is to house things that you like to keep near your bed, such as books, magazines, and the remote control. Put the display items on the top, because they're used most often, and stack the books and magazines down below.

Store hand cream and lip balm in your nightstand drawer.

During the winter months, I go through several tubes of hand cream. But my daughter would always borrow it and my cat would knock it over, so I started to hide it in the drawer. It's easy to locate, and I no longer have to buy replacements!

Use a jewelry box or tree to store rings, earrings, necklaces, and bracelets.

Don't just throw your jewelry on top of the dresser in a tangle, where it can easily fall off! Find a jewelry box with a place to hang necklaces, and organize all your other pieces into groups by type—rings, bracelets, and so on. You can also purchase a decorative jewelry tree, which will let you organize your jewelry while still keeping it on display.

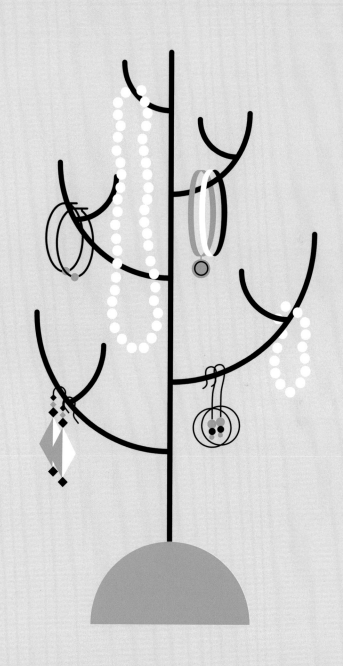

Remove all ill-fitting clothes from your closet.

Come on, we've all got some! It's all right to keep clothes you've grown out of and hope to wear again, but don't fill your closet with them until they actually fit you. Store them in a labeled bag, suitcase, or plastic storage box or put them somewhere where they'll give you incentive.

Put all clothes you no longer wear in a "giveaway" pile.

When you are ready to let go of the clothes you no longer wear, give them to the Goodwill or a local thrift shop. Of course, this goes for your spouse's and kids' clothes, too. Just don't forget to follow through and actually take the clothes to the thrift shop once you've bagged them!

Separate clothes into groups by style.

Laying out clothes the night before is a great way to save time in the morning, and it's easy to do when your closet is organized by style. For example, separate all the long pants, Capri pants, skirts, dresses, and so on. You get the idea!

Use a pants hanger.

If you want to save space in your closet, hang all your pants on a pants hanger. You can easily hang four to six pairs of pants in the space two pairs would require if they were hung separately.

Use a hanger with clips to hang skirts.

These hangers take up less closet space and keep your skirts from getting too wrinkled. It's also easier to choose the one you want to wear when they're all together.

Use a tie rack.

Trying to hang ties and belts from a hanger is useless. They stay on the hanger until you actually place the hanger on the rod, then they all slide off. Save yourself some frustration and install a tie rack on your closet wall.

Hang baseball caps on a hook in the closet.

In our family, we each wear several hats. My husband supports the Red Sox, I am a Yankees fan, and my daughter is somewhere in the middle. I've found that the easiest way to keep all the caps off the floor and doorknobs is to hang them on a hook in the closet.

Use a shoe rack.

Are you tired of searching through piles of mismatched shoes in a dark closet? Instead, use a shoe rack to display your shoes in pairs. It can hang right on the closet door, and will actually allow you to see what you have!

CH

6

BEDROOMS: THEIRS

There is no good reason why kids can't put things back where they belong when their rooms are organized well. When my daughter was born, I endlessly tried to put all the toys back into their original containers, but what a big mistake that was! I wasted more time and space just trying to find homes for everything. I learned my lesson and organized all of her toys, books, and dolls to make them easy to store and keep track of. With these hard-earned tips, you can do the same!

Organize hair accessories in a caddy.

Instead of throwing hair accessories into a dusty bathroom drawer, organize them in a plastic caddy with dividers for separating barrettes, elastics, hair bands, and clips. Children love to pick out their own outfits at a very early age (much earlier than I thought!), and this way they can see all of their hair accessories and quickly choose one before heading off to school.

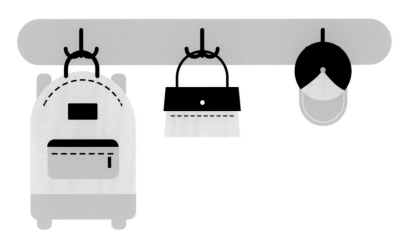

Hang purses and backpacks on a coat hook.
The doorknob can only hold so much! Depending on how many backpacks and purses your children have, you might want to consider mounting a coat hook to hold them. That way they are off the floor and out of the way.

Put all costume jewelry in a box with compartments.
By the age of four, my daughter already had two jewelry boxes full of jewels! Not stored properly, everything gets tangled and it's impossible to sort out. Avoid this disaster by choosing a jewelry box with separate compartments for earrings, necklaces, rings, and bracelets.

Install a hook on the back of the door to hang hats and caps.
Sunhats, baseball caps, spring bonnets, winter hats, and fun character hats crowd lots of kids' closets. To organize them, install one or more hooks on the back of the bedroom door. If you hang the hooks at your child's eye-level, they'll be able to pick and choose themselves.

Clean out old shoes from the closet.
Kids quickly outgrow their shoes. Make sure your child's closet is filled with shoes that are the right size, so that their little toes don't get crunched!

If your child has more than a couple of pairs of shoes, organize them in a shoe rack.
If your child is a budding fashion plate, you might want to put a shoe rack on the closet floor or hang one from the closet door. This way, they'll be able to see everything they have and wear them before their feet grow again!

Store stuffed animals in a basket in the corner.

When my daughter was born, everyone gave her a stuffed bear or bunny or some sort of cuddly thing. When she stopped playing with them, I arranged them in a nice wicker basket in the corner of her room. Even when your child outgrows her stuffed animals, it's nice to keep them around to remind her of the people who so kindly gave them to her.

Store books in a big basket.

I firmly believe that kids who are read to will be readers themselves. Place a book basket in every room so that your child can choose one to read any time it strikes them. And if your kids like to linger in their beds before they get up for the day, put special books in a bedside basket that's easy for kids to reach. They'll keep themselves occupied and you'll get to sleep a little longer!

Install a high shelf to keep special keepsakes out of reach.

Lots of grandparents get enjoyment out of giving their grandkids special collectibles on birthdays and other holidays. In order to make sure these keepsakes will still be collectible when your child is grown, install a shelf on which to display them. Make sure the shelf is out of reach, so dolls and other keepsakes can't get knocked over during a play date.

Put all toys and balls in a toy box.

You can't have too many toy-storage areas! Kids need their own toy storage in their bedrooms, too. Put all toys into a nice toy box that matches their room's decor. Find a toy box that will grow with the kids—one that you can redecorate whenever you redecorate their room.

Clean out their dressers and put all outgrown or out-of-season clothes in a plastic tote.

Kids love to dress themselves, but it's difficult to do when their drawers are crowded with things that don't fit. In order to help your children gain independence in this area, remove all such clothing from their dressers and closets. If you have younger children, nieces, or nephews, put the clothes in a plastic tote for safekeeping. (Otherwise, it's off to the Goodwill!) Be sure to label the tote so you can easily locate it when needed.

Organize underwear, tights, and socks.

It's important to have your child's dresser set up in a way that's easy for him or her to use. This gives him a sense of independence and makes life easier for you. Keep undershirts and underwear together and socks and tights in another drawer.

Put pajamas in another drawer.

Organize the drawer by putting summer pajamas in one pile and winter pajamas in another.

Store "future" clothing in yet another drawer.

Kids grow fast, and it's so nice to have clothes they can grow into. Parents with growing children quickly learn to buy the next size up! Store these clothes in a drawer of their own. Organize separate stacks by size if necessary.

Put kids' dirty clothes in a hamper.
I'm a firm believer in putting a hamper in every bedroom closet. Train your kids to drop their dirty clothes in their hamper, not on the floor, bed, chairs, and every other available surface.

File special vacation pictures in a small album for your child.

The first vacation my daughter remembers is a trip to Sesame Place when she was two years old. I made her a photo album of special memories from that trip, and it helps her to remember the fun we had. Parents go to so much trouble planning special vacations that our children will love, why not make sure they'll have something to remember them by!

Arrange special photos on a fabric memo board and hang it on the wall.

No one has enough space to frame every picture they would like to. A great way to maximize your family picture display is to use a fabric memo board. Stick some favorite pictures under the ribbons, and you can easily change them whenever you're inspired!

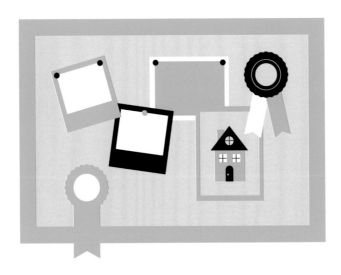

Use plastic sheet covers to preserve special artwork or letters and store them in a separate binder for each child.

Kids put a great deal of effort into making pictures and writing cards. Shouldn't you put a little effort into keeping them intact? Put special pieces in clear plastic sheet covers and file them in a binder to keep these memories organized.

Use an extra-large storage tote as a baby box.

When I was a kid, my parents used an apple box for my baby box. It held my baby pictures, artwork, report cards, and many other memories of my childhood. The box is now worn and filled to the top. Instead of a cardboard box, use an extra-large plastic storage tote with a cover for a baby box. In it, you can keep his or her baby book and first pair of shoes, and there is enough space to store all report cards and artwork until senior year of high school! A plastic tote with a cover will protect your cherished memories, and it's easy to keep it neatly organized. Make sure you put a label with each child's name on his or her box.

Make regular entries to your child's baby book.

Many baby books go up to age five! Every now and then, take a few minutes to jot down a special memory in your child's baby book. If you do it a little bit at a time, it won't seem so overwhelming.

Fill out a Kinderprint ID card for your child.

It's scary to think about, but it's better to be safe than sorry. Fill out a Kinderprint ID card for your child so you have all their personal information and a current picture readily available.

Store all necessary school items in a backpack and hang it in their rooms.

You pack for overnight trips the night before, so why not pack for school the night before? It'll save you time in the morning when you *really* need it. Keep everything your kids will need at school in their backpacks, so their stuff is ready to go when they are.

Store dance items in a tote bag.

A leotard and tights can easily be lost in mountains of laundry. Try to keep them separate, and after you wash them, put them back into your child's dance bag so they are ready for the next class.

Store all beach accessories in large tote bag or bucket.

Spontaneity is part of summer! Keep all beach toys in a big tote bag or beach bucket so they're ready to go when the sun starts sizzling.

Keep storage bins or baskets in the mudroom to store winter gear.

Winter represents a whole set of organization challenges. There is extra dirt from boots and layers upon layers of clothing. Put a little basket or bin in your mudroom for each child to keep his or her mittens, hat, scarf, and winter boots.

Prominently hang a calendar that clearly lists chores.

It's never too early to get your children organized! Kids need a sense of order in their lives—it gives them stability. Make a calendar with everyone's name and chores in different colors of ink.

CH

7

MAKING THE HOME
OFFICE WORK

t's easy to create a messy work environment—and even easier to close the door and walk away. I know some people claim to work better in chaos, but I don't believe it. I have a need for clean and that includes the office. If you treat it like any other room in the house and neaten it up daily, it won't get out of control. A neat, attractive home office will boost your spirits, and you'll finally be able to find anything in seconds. Why work in a sty? Needless to say, you can use these tips in your "real" office, too.

Use a large calendar to organize family events.

It's not easy juggling work and family, but you can be organized! If you like to visualize the month ahead with a paper calendar, hang a large one on the wall to keep track of family events such as sports schedules, parties, and school events.

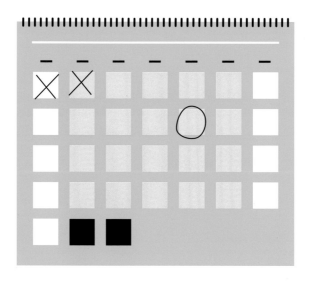

Organize greeting cards by holiday inside a Pendeflex folder.

It's always a good idea to have extra greeting cards on hand for birthdays, anniversaries, and holidays. It's hard to remember the dates until you see it on Facebook the day of or flip the calendar page and by then, it's too late! If you have cards on hand, store them in a Pendeflex folder so they won't become bent and wrinkled. You don't want anyone to think his or her card has been lying around for months!

Note birthdays and special events on your calendar for the entire year.

Every January 1st, I sit down with a cup of coffee and my calendars, one for the year that just ended and one for the year beginning. I go through my old calendar and write down every birthday and anniversary in my new calendar. By doing this, you'll just need to take a quick glance at your calendar to be reminded of special occasions. Or add birthdays and special events to your digital calendars and mark them as yearly occurrences so you don't have to enter them ever again.

Keep track of user manuals and warranty information.

While YouTube videos are pretty helpful when you're familiarizing yourself with a new gadget, it is always nice to reference the instruction manual that comes with a device. Store all user manuals, and accompanying warranty information, in a binder so that you know right where to go if something goes wrong and who to contact if you need more help.

Store important documents and valuables in a safe place.

Keep all your important documents, such as marriage and birth certificates, passports, and titles of ownership in a safe place. A safe deposit box at the bank or a fireproof safe in your home is a good choice for this. Better to be safe than sorry!

Arrange your desk in a way that works for *you*.
Your workspace should function how you need it to function. If you do a lot of writing, be sure to leave a large area empty. If you scan a lot of documents, clear a space for your scanner. Whatever your situation calls for, be sure your desk space is optimized.

Remove all unnecessary supplies from your desk.
Desks are often cluttered with many supplies you don't need on a daily basis. Keep them in a drawer or storage closet, and give yourself space to work!

Organize papers in a stackable tray.
Every office has loose papers floating around, and they just add to the chaos, allowing important notifications and bills get lost. Take advantage of vertical space with stackable trays, and leave your desk space free for work. If you label your stackable trays, you'll know what's coming in and what's going out.

Mount two shelving brackets and a shelf to store books and binders.
Elevate your office! Install a shelf above your desk and organize your books by size. Use bookends so the books don't come tumbling down when someone slams the door.

Put loose paperclips in a magnetic storage box.
Office supply stores sell paperclips in big boxes that take up too much space on the desk. Use a small magnetic box to keep paperclips from spilling all over the place, and put the rest of them in your office storage closet.

Store pens, pencils, and scissors in a tall glass or jar on your desktop.
It's often difficult to store all of your writing utensils in the top desk drawer because it isn't meant to hold twenty pens, pencils, and highlighters. Keep a nice glass or jar on top of your desk for writing utensils, so they will be neatly contained and easily accessible. Depending on the size of the container, you might have room for scissors, too!

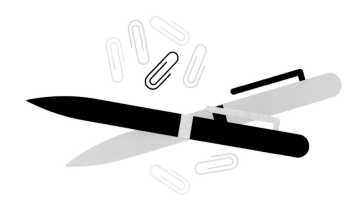

Stow extra pens, pencils, and highlighters in a small plastic tote.
If you have a storage closet, you can store all of your extra writing utensils in a clear plastic tote on a shelf. Label the front of the tote so they'll be easy to find.

Store clipboards, writing pads, and stationery in a large plastic tote.
Most pads come in packs of ten or more, so keep extra ones in a large plastic tote in your storage closet. Be sure to label the tote so people know where to find more paper without having to ask you.

Make a list of low-inventory items.
To avoid a hurried trip to your local office supply store, keep an ongoing shopping list on your desk. When you run low on things, simply grab your list and go! Another option is to order online before your supplies run out, that way a backup is already at your home when you need it.

File folders alphabetically.

If you still work with hard copy printouts, it's much quicker to find information in an organized file cabinet. If you alphabetize your file folders, you'll save yourself time and aggravation. If you strictly work digitally, your computer will do the alphabetizing legwork for you, or you can put a number at the beginning of your file name if you want the folders to appear in a certain order.

Clean out your filing cabinets and digitize what you can.

It's very hard to locate a document in an overstuffed file cabinet. Clean out the drawers and pack last year's information in a labeled storage box. If you want to go the extra mile and completely clear your space from clutter, scan documents and save the files to your personal computer or to the cloud. This way, you can access them from anywhere and print copies if you need to.

Delete documents you no longer need on your computer.

Regardless of the amount of memory your computer stores, you don't want to have a cluttered "My Documents" folder. Delete all the documents you no longer need, such as old resumes, letters, and college papers. If you do want to keep them, save space on your device by uploading them to cloud storage.

Clear your digital desktop.

When was the last time you updated the icons on your desktop? Having too many links, documents, and programs can really crowd your desktop screen and make your laptop difficult to navigate. Delete old links and documents and organize the items you want to keep into folders in your browser or in the "Documents" tab.

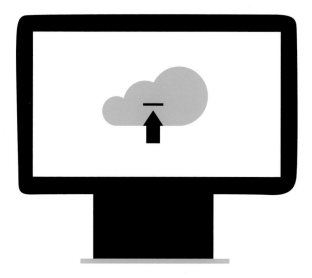

Back up your devices.

Has your computer ever been affected by a virus? Ever lost your smartphone? If so, you understand the importance of backing up your data to a secure account in the cloud or to an external hard drive. Set up auto-backup on your devices or do a manual backup on a regular basis. That way, you don't have to think about it, and you know you're covered should anything happen.

Set reminders on your devices for time-sensitive events.

Pop-up reminders are a great way to keep track of tasks that require immediate action. That way, you see the task at hand every time you check your phone or laptop. For example, if you don't have your accounts billed automatically, setting a monthly or yearly reminder could save you from late fees.

Clean out your email.

Sort through email on a weekly basis to remove old correspondence or unnecessary emails from subscriber lists. By doing so, you'll also get a reminder of things that need immediate attention—you can even flag or star those emails as important.

Respond to emails promptly.

We all check our email several times a day, but are we always quick to respond? To avoid a message getting pushed down in your inbox, be sure to reply right away or, at the very least, flag it as important so it catches your eye later.

Scan business cards.

Businesses are doing their best to go green, but one feature that's not really phasing out is business cards. There are plenty of apps and online organizers to help you scan business cards and store the information digitally. So, as soon as you're handed a card, scan it, upload the info, and recycle the card. No more misplacing the contact information of someone in your expanding network.

Streamline your contacts list.

It can be handy to save addresses, phone numbers, and emails in your contacts list, but old addresses and outdated contact information can take up unnecessary space on your devices. Once a year, de-clutter your digital space by deleting contact information that you never use. If you still have an actual address book or have information written down on a piece of paper, transfer them to your phone or laptop, or discard them if they are out-of-date.

Organize your phone's home screen.

Just like your laptop, your smartphone's home screen or main menu can easily become cluttered with apps. Take the time to delete apps you downloaded for a one-time purpose or ones that came with your phone and you never use. You can also organize apps into folders by category and move your most-used apps into a place you can access them quickly, such as the home screen bar of an iPhone or the dock of an Android.

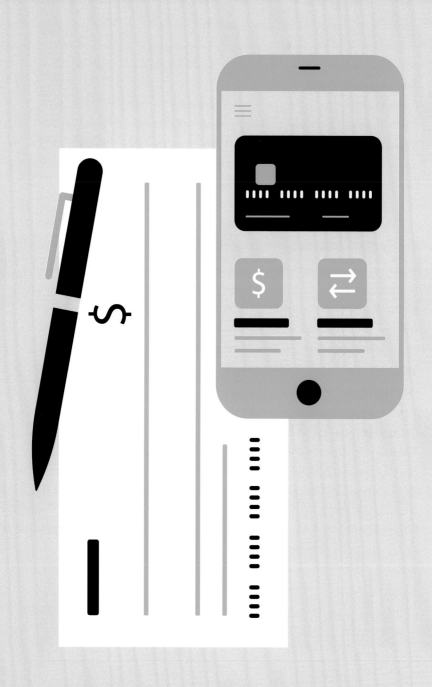

Balance your checkbook and check your mobile banking apps.
If you still use a checkbook, it's important to reconcile it every month. An easy way to keep track of the funds flowing in and out of your accounts is through mobile banking apps. You can check your account balance, see when people cash checks, and view your transactions. Some banks even send out instantaneous notifications whenever there is action on your account.

Use a different-colored pen to balance your checkbook.
If you still write checks, use a pen with different-colored ink so that you can focus on the current month's transactions. You won't have to keep fumbling through deposits and withdrawals, trying to figure out which ones are current.

Pay bills promptly or set up automatic payments.
Don't let bills sit until they're due. Pay them on a timely basis, not only to maintain your good credit score but also to de-clutter your desk! As mentioned before, a convenient way to make sure your bills are paid on time is to set up automatic payments. This way, you don't even have to worry about whether you paid them or not!

Make a list of monthly expenses.

Before you prepare a yearly budget, you have to know your monthly expenses. Be sure to include car loans, credit card loans, mortgage or lease payments, office supplies, bills (cell phone, Internet, streaming services, etc.), gym memberships, clothing, gas, meals, and any other expenses you may encounter on a regular basis. You can find budget templates online, or there are several reputable apps that help you track and manage your spending.

Make a list of yearly expenses.

Once you know your monthly expenses, it's easy to determine your yearly expenses. Make sure to include all charitable donations and P.O. Box or safety deposit box renewal fees.

Create a twelve-month budget.

At the end of each year, create a twelve-month budget for the following year, and revise it as necessary. Be sure that your budget is feasible and allows for unexpected expenses.

Calculate credit card interest rates.

Credit card companies will compete for your business as long as you have a decent credit score. Make sure your cards have low interest rates, and if not, contact other companies to inquire about what they can offer you. If another company offers a lower rate, it might be smart to consolidate your cards and receive just one bill every month.

Make a list of all credit card balances and interest rates to determine a payoff schedule.

Many people fall into debt traps, and it becomes very difficult to climb out! Make a list of all your debts, the interest rates, and the life of the loan. That way, you can determine what you should focus on, and what should be paid off first.

TIPS FOR THE WORK OFFICE

Whether you actually work out of your home or you'd just like an organized office at work, these tips will help you reduce the clutter.

Clear your voicemail box.

No business comes in when your voicemail is full. Delete old messages and return important calls so your voicemail is always available for new messages.

Sort through customer files.

If you send regular mailings to your customers, don't waste time or money sending them to inactive customers. Assign different codes to your customers so you know if there was a problem or they just haven't used your goods or services in a while.

Update customer contact information.

When business is slow, scan your customer files and make sure all contact information is up to date. If something is missing, contact your customers and ask them to provide you with current home, work, and cell phone numbers, and a current address.

Clear your bulletin or white board of old information.

Sometimes it's nice to have a non-digital way to keep track of important tasks. If you use a bulletin or white board to display pertinent information regarding jobs, appointments, or meetings, be sure to keep it clean and up-to-date.

Get payroll materials organized prior to payday.

While many companies use automated payroll services, and even more employees opt for direct deposit, it's still important to be organized and punctual when dealing with people's livelihoods. Particularly if you hand-deliver paychecks. Prepare anything you may need for payday the day before. After all, a paid employee is a happy employee!

Document anniversary dates for each employee.

All employees need to feel valued, and want you to recognize their accomplishments. A simple way to do this is to acknowledge the anniversary of their starting date. Set yearly calendar events on your device or write down every employee's anniversary date on your calendar at the beginning of each year and mark the occasion with a card, cake, flowers, or another token of your appreciation.

Type meeting notes and distribute a copy to each employee.
Make sure your employees are kept in the loop and everyone is on the same page by sending out weekly meeting notes.

File meeting notes by topic or by date.
If you run an office out of your home, the last thing you need is more clutter! Store office copies of meeting notes and safety handouts in a large binder in chronological order. It's out of the way, but accessible should you need it. Even better, go paperless and create a folder on your computer desktop or on the cloud to store these things.

Update your appointment calendar.
It's so important to keep an accurate record of meetings and appointments. Everyone gets bogged down between home and work, and you don't want to forget something vital. When booking an appointment, fill in all the details of the meeting, including your contact's address and telephone number.

8

LAUNDRY
ROOM LOGIC

A laundry room is where things get cleaned, not dirtied. Apply that concept to the room itself and tidy up!

Store laundry detergent and stain remover on a shelf above the washer and dryer.

Set up a laundry station to streamline the laundering process. I use an old shelf that was once in my bedroom. It keeps everything at eye level.

Keep a laundry bag or hamper in the laundry room.

You're right, I *did* tell you to put a hamper in all your bedroom closets, too. By putting one in the laundry room you can transfer dirty clothes between washings. And if your laundry room's located near your kitchen, you can toss dishtowels, dust rags, and the like in the laundry-room hamper until wash day.

Hang wet clothes on a two- or three-tiered drying rack.

Wet clothes dry faster if they're hung properly instead of strewn over a chair. Invest in a multi-tiered drying rack so you can dry an entire load at once. It's perfect for delicate lingerie, wools, nylons, socks, and other fragile items you don't want to put in the dryer. It's also a great place to finish drying those thick towels that come out of the dryer still damp.

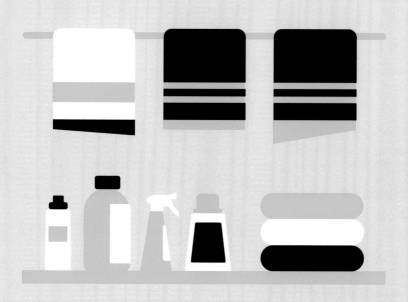

Keep a mending/ironing pile in a basket next to the ironing board.

I never understood why my mother kept a laundry basket full of clothes under the ironing board until I started taking care of my own wardrobe. If you put clothes that need attention in a basket instead of back into the closet, you won't waste time putting together a faulty outfit. No one wants to be rushing out the door, only to find that their shirt is missing a button!

Hang a closet rod above the washer and dryer.

If you already have shelves on the wall in your laundry room, you can make great use of the space above your washer and dryer by attaching a closet rod. Keep a supply of plastic hangers, and you can hang up wrinkle-prone items the second you take them from the dryer. Ironing may soon be but a memory!

Put a bookcase in your laundry room.

Here's one last thought about shelves. Because laundering involves so many supplies—detergents, bleaches, fabric softeners, stain-removal sheets, and so on—storage shelves are essential. If you have room for it and don't want to hang shelves on the wall, a sturdy, moisture-proof bookcase is ideal. (A white bookcase in a white laundry room is a nice touch.) You can store all your laundering supplies, extra toilet paper and tissues, and even a few books!

Keep weekly cleaning items in a caddy so it's easily accessible.
Try to keep weekly cleaning supplies, such as furniture polish and glass
cleaner, in a central location, such as the laundry room. Store these supplies
in a caddy that you can move around the house as you're cleaning.

Store surplus cleaning supplies in a storage crate.
Bigger is better—at least that's what we're told. Instead of buying one tub
of cleaning wipes, buy three and save a dime. I am guilty of doing this, and
know that storing them in one place is next to impossible. Keep your surplus
cleaning supplies in a plastic storage crate on your laundry-room floor. They'll
be there when you need them and won't be crowding your cabinet.

CH

9

STORAGE
SOLUTIONS

W rapping paper, decorations, craft supplies—yikes! All too often,
these things end up crammed into closets, under the stairs, in the
basement or attic—impossible to find it when you need them!

Crafts are almost a category in and of themselves. If you're like me, you
enjoy taking up new hobbies and giving away or selling the fruits of your
labors. It can be difficult to store craft materials so that they don't become
wrinkled and tangled, but I've found a way!

Store beading supplies in clear plastic tackle boxes.
You can keep thousands of beads organized and contained in the type of clear, flat plastic boxes that are used to store fishing lures and hardware such as nails and screws. The boxes have lots of dividers, stack for easy storage, and you can see what's in them at a glance!

Store craft supplies in clear plastic shoeboxes.
Plastic shoeboxes make tidy, stackable storage containers for craft supplies. They're easy to carry around, and you won't need to open every box to see what's inside.

Use plastic stackable drawers to store sewing and knitting materials.
If a roll of thread comes unraveled, it is very difficult to roll it up without knotting it. Store all your knitting and sewing materials in stackable drawers to keep them contained. Be sure to keep your needles stored safely so they don't fall into the wrong hands!

Store rubber-stamping materials in a plastic tote with a handle.
When I got into rubber stamping, everyone wanted a lesson! I use a great storage container with a handle and lid, which makes it is easy to lug around. Even if you're not teaching stamping on the road, it's a great place to store your materials until you're ready to use them.

Store cake-decorating tips and couplings in a plastic storage bag.
Metal tips and couplings are easier to use than plastic icing tubes, and they produce a better decoration. After you wash the tips and couplings, keep them in a plastic storage bag so that none of the pieces get lost.

Store wrapping paper rolls in a large tote, bucket, or basket, so they don't unwind or get wrinkled.

Who wants to walk into a party and present someone with a wrinkled gift? Not me! Store your wrapping paper rolls in a tote or other tall container. Be sure to roll them tightly before placing them in the container.

Store your ribbons, bows, gift tags, tape, and scissors in a bag and put it in your wrapping container.

Keep all of your wrapping items together so everything you need will be at your fingertips. Put your tape, scissors, and package decorations in a bag, and keep it in the top of your wrapping-paper tote, bucket, or basket.

Tape the ends of ribbon to the roll so they don't get unraveled.

Have you ever purchased a big roll of ribbon with four or five different colors on it? I thought this was a great idea until I tried to put it away. What a mess! Tape the end of each color (or roll) to keep your ribbons neat and accessible.

Store ornaments in egg cartons.

I prefer the double-topped plastic kind, but cardboard egg cartons work fine, too. If you have as many ornaments as I do, stack the cartons in a labeled cardboard box for safekeeping.

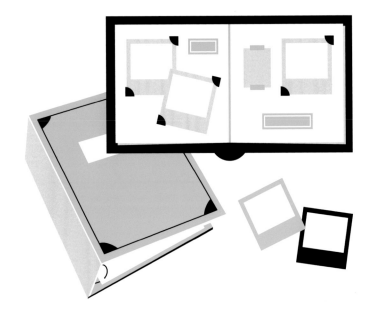

Keep scrapbook materials in a large binder with pocket sheets.
Proper storage of scrapbook materials such as papers, frames, and inserts, is essential to creating a neat and clean piece of art. If you organize a binder with pocket sheets for all your supplies, they'll stay crisp and unwrinkled for your next project.

Write names and dates on pictures and store them in a photo album.

My parents raised seven children and barely had time to breathe, never mind organize family photos! My mother started the "picture drawer," and every picture was filed there with or without a name and a date. It probably seemed like a good idea at the time, but it certainly isn't easy to find something now! If you write the names and dates on your pictures as you get them printed, and put them into an album for safekeeping, your memories will be alive and organized. I use a new album every year, and label the outside of it with the date so I know just where to look for a certain picture.

Store digital photos in albums in the cloud or on an external hard drive.

If scrapbooking is not your thing or if you have too many photos on your devices to print, it is still beneficial to organize them and make sure they are saved in multiple locations. Start by categorizing your photos by subject or date and saving these photos to a secure account in the cloud or onto an external hard drive. This way, if a device is lost or stolen, your memories won't be gone as well. You can also organize your photos in a more artistic way through digital scrapbooks offered on various photo-printing websites.

10

THE GARBAGE-FREE
GARAGE

Even though the garage may seem like the perfect place to let go, it can be easily organized in a few simple steps. Even my husband admits it's nice to have room to put our cars in the garage! Try these tips to transform your garage into a place for cars *and* storage.

Use hooks to hang rakes, shovels, and ladders.

Keep your ladders and landscape-maintenance tools on sturdy hooks mounted on the wall. No more tripping over them!

Hang ceiling hooks for bicycles and strollers.

If you want room to park your car, hang big items such as bikes and strollers from the ceiling of your garage. It's amazing how much floor space this frees up!

Use rafters to store sleds.

Rafters or an upper level in your garage, storage shed, or barn, are extremely useful for storing sleds, toboggans, and other large seasonal items, such as surfboards.

Hang snow tires on hose mounts.

Mount a few garden-hose holders on your garage wall—they're the perfect size to hold a tire. You can hang up your snow tires in warm weather and your regular tires come winter.

Store all toys in a large plastic tote with cover.

Store all outside toys such as balls, bats, and Frisbees in an extra-large plastic tote. It's a great way to keep your yard from looking like a playground.

Use a shelving unit to store tools and gardening supplies.

If you don't have a workbench to store your tools, a shelving unit works perfectly. Keep all small tools such as hammers, mallets, and saws, off the floor and away from children. Shelves are also a great place to store your gardening supplies. But if you have mice, it is wise to hang your gardening gloves.

Store auto supplies in a shelving unit.

Put those bottles of antifreeze, window-washing fluid, oil, and the like on shelves, where they'll stay tidy and accessible but out of your child's reach.

Store fasteners in a storage bin.

Have you gotten a tetanus shot lately? If not, you may want to grab those nails and screws (very carefully!) and put them in a safe place such as a storage tray. Organize all fasteners in a plastic tray with dividers so you can separate them by type.

Put an umbrella stand by the door.

Keep those dripping umbrellas out by placing an umbrella stand in the garage by the door to the house. This keeps unwanted moisture out of your house and allows your umbrellas to dry properly.

Place a "shoe mat" by the door.

Put a doormat in the garage by the connecting door, and train your family to take off their wet or muddy shoes before entering the house. No more dirty footsteps all over your clean kitchen floor!

PART TWO

Entertaining

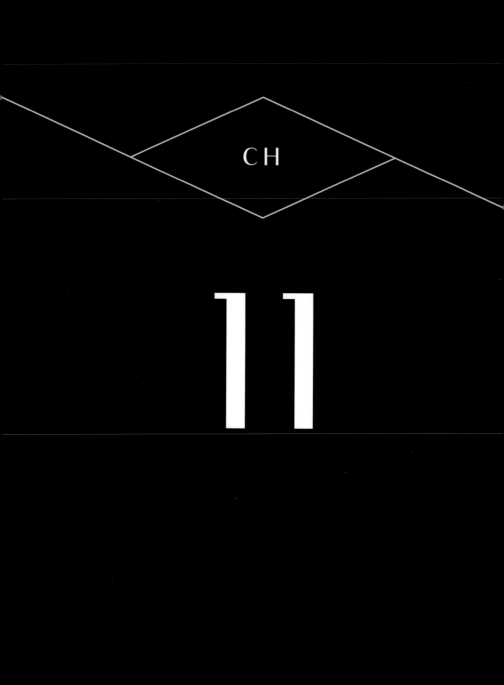

CH

11

HAVOC-LESS
HOLIDAYS

H oliday gatherings can be big, little, or somewhere in between. This is one time when size doesn't matter, but details do! These tips will allow you to host a holiday party and actually enjoy it, too.

Keep a greeting card list.

If you send greeting cards or family letters, keep a list of names and addresses from year to year. Keep it on your computer, so you can easily update it when necessary. This can also double as your holiday party invitation list—give or take a few names to account for those who live far away or are more of an acquaintance.

Decide what type of party you're hosting.

Before you go any further, what type of party will it be? A cocktail party, dinner party, or open house? It's important to make a decision early, because it might influence the guest list and will definitely influence menu choices and the time of day, not to mention wardrobe!

Make a guest list with spaces for responses.

You can do this by hand or on a spreadsheet. Make four columns for names, addresses, phone numbers, and their response. Mark the responses in different colors so you can get a quick tally. (For example, yes in green and no in red.)

Plan an activity to make the get-together fun!

It's always fun to have an activity that draws people together, especially during the holidays when some people need a mood makeover. If you are so inclined, invite people to a tree-trimming party or to go caroling after a dinner party. It will boost spirits and get people in the holiday mood! Be sure to note the activity in the invitations so people come prepared.

Send invitations six weeks before the party.

If you send out invitations early, people can mark down the date of your party before receiving other invitations. You'll have a better turnout.

Ask guests to RSVP two weeks ahead of time.

It's important, especially during the holiday season, to have an accurate head count for a party. Regardless of what type of party it is, you need to plan for enough food and drink to keep people happy. Anticipate people getting caught up in the hustle and bustle of the holidays, and ask for responses a bit earlier than you need them. That way, by the time you go shopping, everyone who plans to come should have gotten a hold of you.

Include an end time for your party in the invitation.

If you're having a party in the evening, you'll want to include an end time so people don't linger until the early morning hours. With a few drinks and lively conversation, it might be hard for some guests to leave!

Have a list of food you can delegate, if given the opportunity.
Make a list of easy-to-prepare foods that guests can bring. Keep this list by your RSVP list, so you can readily suggest something if someone offers to help.

Get out every recipe you'll need.
Once you've collected your recipes, make sure you have all of the ingredients. It's no fun to stop in the middle of cooking and run to the store for a key ingredient!

Make a shopping list of ingredients.
If you don't have all the ingredients on hand, make a list of what you need so you can get in and out of the store quickly. Don't waste time wandering the aisles.

Try out new recipes ahead of time.
My mother-in-law taught me this, and it's paid off tenfold! Sometimes recipes can get tricky, and you don't want to be faced with disaster on the eve of your party. You can apply this practice to cake decorating too, as I have every year for my daughter's birthday. Remember, practice makes perfect!

Make cookies ahead of time and store them in the freezer.

Most cookies freeze well, and guests will never know the difference.

Put holiday cookies on a tiered cookie plate to save space and keep flavors separated.

You don't want chocolate cookies smeared with jelly from the linzer tarts! If you use a cookie plate with two or three tiers, you can put out more cookies and won't have to replenish them as often.

Decorate the house a week or so before the party.

I like to decorate for Christmas the weekend after Thanksgiving, but that might not be a good idea if your party is at the end of December! Evergreens should look fresh, not to mention that it becomes dangerous to wrap decorative lights around dry foliage.

Rearrange furniture if necessary.

We had some friends who always moved their living room furniture around to make room for their Christmas tree. It seemed ridiculous to me at first, but why not? Most living room furniture is easy to move, and it's always nice to have open spaces where guests can visit and not feel claustrophobic.

Fill the house with holiday plants.

Don't bother buying flower arrangements for a holiday party, because they won't last long. Instead, fill your house with poinsettias, cyclamen, and decorated Norfolk Island pines to make it look festive and colorful. Two added benefits: You can set them up well ahead of time (as long as you remember to water them!), and, if you like, you can give them to guests at the end of the party.

Provide decorative paper hand towels in the bathroom for guests.
It's nice to provide your guests with personal hand towels, rather than asking them to share one with the other guests. Paper hand towels can be discarded after your guests use them, so you won't have extra laundry to do and your bathroom will stay tidy.

String lights on the bushes and walkway in front of your house so guests can easily spot the party.
It gets dark early in December, so add a little light. The little white lights now come in a convenient netted form, so you can just toss the netting over a bush, plug it in, and voila! Evenly spaced lights look so beautiful and festive; you may just want to leave them up all year!

Make party favors simple.
If you're going to give out party favors, put them together ahead of time. Choose something simple, such as a nice bottle of wine in a decorative wine sack or an ornament in a silk bag. Display them in a basket by the door, and give one to each couple as they're leaving.

Set up a beverage area and a food area.

Set up two separate areas, so people aren't tripping over each other as they go for a drink or a bite to eat.

Stock the beverage area the night before.

Obviously, you wouldn't put out chilled beverages the night before, but you can set out all the liquor and wine that will be served at room temperature.

Set up the punch bowl and serving bowls the night before.

Chances are that you don't often use your punch bowl. Am I right? If so, get it out the night before and wash it to get rid of those dust bunnies!

Set the dinner table the night before.

Whether you're hosting a formal dinner party or a casual open house, put the plates, glasses, and flatware out the night before. You'll have more time on party day for the inevitable last-minute preparations.

Have snacks ready for people who drop in.
Have some quick snacks ready to whip out if someone drops in unexpectedly during party preparation. Keep cheese, crackers, and cut veggies and dip on hand so you can put together a quick platter.

Make up cookie plates as last-minute gifts.
Regardless of how many times you review your gift list, there will always be the one you didn't count on! Arrange some homemade cookies on decorative plates or in tins so that you're not caught empty-handed.

Put decorative sugar cubes in a bowl for coffee and tea.
Sugar cubes are fancy and fun to use, and they don't leave a mess all over your tablecloth the way granulated sugar does. You may even be able to find holiday sugar cubes with holly, wreaths, and Christmas trees on them! Don't forget to set out a sugar spoon, too.

Pre-slice pies and cakes.

As long as your pie or cake won't fall apart on you, this is a great idea. The slices will all be the same size (more or less), and you can either serve them or set them on a buffet table for guests to easily serve themselves.

Set out desserts near the coffee maker.

Keep desserts, dessert plates, and coffee cups and saucers near your coffee maker so that all the dessert essentials are together. This will also help you remember to turn on the coffee maker when you're serving dessert! And if people are assisting you in the kitchen, they can easily tell what needs to go out when everything is grouped together.

Keep track of gifts so you can easily write thank-you notes.
Most people will enter your home with a bottle of wine or some other type of hostess gift. Keep track of this, so you can send your guests thank-you notes after the party. Keep the gifts together with their cards or write down the gift and giver on a note pad.

Cut greeting cards and use them as gift tags.
Recycle your greeting cards by making them into gift tags for next year's presents. They'll look nicer than any self-stick label you can buy!

Keep unwanted gifts for future gift giving.
If someone gives you something that you'll never use in a million years, or you already have three of, don't fret. Keep those gifts in or near your wrapping tub so they'll be on hand when it's time for a gift. Someday, somewhere, someone will be happy to receive them! But here's a word to the wise: Make sure you tag the gifts with the names of the original givers to avoid a future *faux pas*.

Queue up a holiday playlist.

Shuffle is a great thing! Download a holiday playlist or create your own on your phone or laptop so that there is something for everyone, and you don't need to attend to the music all night long.

Designate an area for kids to hang out.

If you've invited children to the party, make sure there is a place for them to play games and watch television. If young children will attend, set out coloring supplies, puzzles, and books to keep them occupied.

Turn down the heat a few hours before the party.

People tend to turn up the heat when it's cold outside, but don't do that if a hundred people are coming into your home. Remember, bodies produce heat—and you don't want sweaty guests! This is especially true if you plan to build a fire.

Build a fire in the fireplace an hour before the party.

If you weren't a boy scout, it might be wise to start a fire early well before the guests arrive! Getting a good blaze going early gives you time to clean up any spilled wood chips or ashes.

Have plastic containers ready for guests to take home leftovers.

Buy some inexpensive disposable plastic containers and wash them so they're ready to go home with your guests. This is a great way to help clean up the kitchen!

CH

12

HOUSEGUESTS
WELCOME

I f you want your guests to return, make them comfortable. (If you don't want them to return, well, that's a different story entirely.) Think back to a time when you felt happy and at home as a guest in someone's house, and try to recreate that feeling. A little planning goes a long way.

Clean the guestroom and make the bed.

It's nice for your guests to have the comforts of home while they're away. If you know what kind of bedding they like, make sure your guestroom bed is made up that way. Know someone hates flannel sheets? When they come to visit, be sure to make up the guest bed with crisp cotton sheets. Have a visitor who loves being cozy? Leave some slippers at the foot of the bed.

Make sure there are hangers in the closet.

Ideally, a guestroom closet would be empty and reserved for guests. However, that's never the case. Guestroom closets get filled with linens, seasonal clothes, and other things you don't want crowding your own closet. Before your guests arrive, neaten up their closet and make sure they are able to hang their clothes if they choose to. You might want to leave the closet door ajar so they feel welcome to use it.

Make sure the guest nightstand has all the essentials.

Everyone has their own bedtime routine, but there are a few common necessities. Set up the nightstand with a clock, some tissues, a small bottle of hand cream, and a coaster.

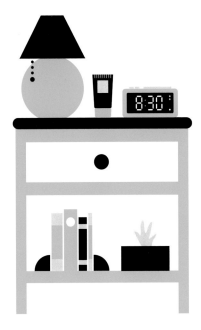

Make up a basket with bottled water, crackers, and fruit for the guest room.

No guest wants to admit that dinner was just simply not enough! Put your guests at ease by leaving a basketful of snacks in their room.

Put extra pillows on the guestroom bed.

Lots of people like to sleep with two pillows, but no one wants to be a nuisance and ask for more. Make sure your guests have plenty of pillows in their room. At the very least, the bed will look plump and comfy!

Put extra blankets at the foot of the bed.

Some like it hot! You certainly don't want your guests freezing all night, so provide them with extra covers, even if the room feels warm to you.

Ask your guests for information on any food allergies or dislikes.
You don't want to spend an hour preparing a meal that your guests won't eat.
If you've never been host to these particular guests, make a point of asking
them of their preferences and dietary restrictions. You can then focus your
efforts on preparing a meal that everyone will enjoy.

Plan meals and make a shopping list.
Once you know what your guests like and dislike, make a menu for each
day they'll be visiting. Make a shopping list so you can get in and out of the
store quickly.

Make meals ahead of time.
Dinners are easy to make ahead of time and freeze. Some items that freeze
well are lasagna, meatloaf, and homemade macaroni and cheese. Put the
main dish in the oven, slice some nice bread, throw together a salad, and
voila! A hassle-free, home cooked meal for your guests.

Prepare breakfast the night before.
Breakfast is the most important meal of the day, so put some effort into
preparing it ahead of time. Make a breakfast casserole, and get up early to
put it into the oven so that it's done when everyone wakes up. Cut up some
fresh fruit the night before to balance out the meal. If you don't want to do
something that labor-intensive, make a loaf of banana bread the day before
or get some bagels to go with the fresh fruit.

Stock your guest bathroom with towels, soap, lotion, and toothpaste.
Make sure that your guests have everything they need when they arrive, so they don't have to disturb you at night or in the early morning. If there's a guest shower, set out shampoo and conditioner. Don't forget tissues and toilet paper!

Find out what time your guests will arrive and depart.
Everyone is busy, and you can't waste a day waiting for someone to arrive. Ask your guests what time they plan to arrive and depart, so you can plan your days accordingly.

When your guests arrive, show them where everything is.
My house is your house! Make guests feel at home by welcoming them to grab a snack or cup of coffee without asking you first. Be sure to show them where things are stored, such as extra towels and toilet paper.

Set the timer on the coffee maker.
It's very awkward to be up before your hosts and have to wait around for them to prepare breakfast. Set up the coffee maker so that it's ready to go when they are.

Set up a tray on the kitchen counter with sugar, a pitcher, and spoons.

Once you've set the timer, set up a little coffee station. Include spoons, sugar, artificial sweetener packets, and a cream pitcher. If your guests prefer tea, leave out a few tea bags and fill the kettle with water so they just have to turn on the stove.

Find out if there are any special activities in or around your town.

Depending on the season, there may be something going on that will interest your guests. Check out regional blogs or community event calendars online ahead of time to plan a special outing.

Give yourself a day off.

Organize something for your guests to do one day, so you can have a little down time during their visit. It is okay to plan a little excursion for your guests, and it might be just what they want too. You'll get to play catchup on your everyday business or even just relax for a little while.

CH

13

PARTIES: YOURS

Parties can be fun, or they can be stressful, and the difference is often in the details. Plan your parties so they're fun and easy for *you*, as well as for your guests. Of course, planning an office party can make or break you, so you need to do it right. Forgetting something vital when all eyes are on you can be career suicide. Start with a list and go from there!

Make a to-do list in "countdown order."

Make that list and check it twice to be sure that it's in chronological order. You'll be much less likely to forget something!

Store party information in a folder on your computer.

The key to party planning is organization! Start with a folder on your laptop to keep all pertinent information, such as menus, contracts, the guest list, and contact information. This way, you can store different document formats and keep all the party elements separate. There are also plenty of apps that can help you stay organized with your event.

Make a timeline.

Once you have your list of things to do, draw a timeline and include time estimates for each task. Don't underestimate how long each task will take, either! It will be easier to accomplish with realistic expectations.

Delegate responsibilities.

Okay, this may be the hard part. It may be awkward to ask someone for help, but often some people are just waiting for you to ask. Start off slow by discussing menu or party preparation and asking for their advice. You may be surprised at their response!

Plan your party menu.

Once you've determined the type of party you're having, start on the menu. Make a list of what you'll need and when it needs to be prepared so you can create a timeline.

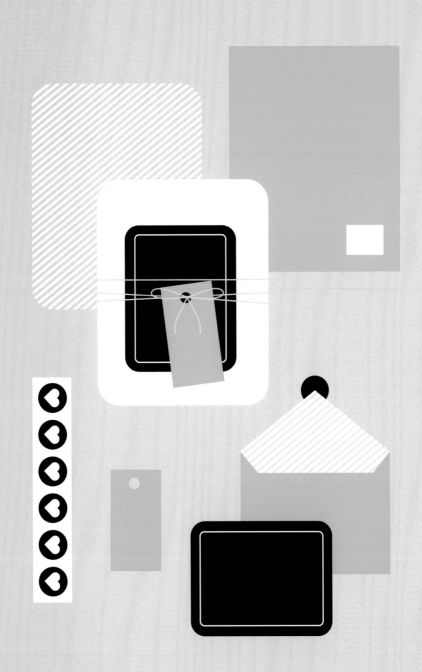

Include directions with the invitations.

Although most people have navigation systems in their cars or GPS capability on their phones, it is a good idea to include directions with invitations for guests who may not have a smartphone or in case of technological malfunction. Instead of verbally repeating the directions a hundred times, include them in the invitations, whether you send them in the mail or online.

Clearly define the hours of the party.

Don't leave an invitation open-ended unless you want guests to hang out until all hours. It would be rude to ask them to leave, so don't invite them to stay unless you want them to!

Ask people to RSVP two weeks in advance.

Two weeks may seem like a long time, but you need as much time as possible to prepare the perfect party. You want an accurate head count, especially if there are gifts to be presented or handouts to be distributed.

Include an email address so guests don't have to call to respond to the invitation.

It's quicker to send an email or text to someone than it is to reply via phone and risk getting into a lengthy conversation. If you make it easy, you'll probably have a better response rate. It also makes it easier for you to go from your email to update your guest list spreadsheet.

Make easy-to-eat foods for a cocktail party or for appetizers.
For a cocktail party, food on a stick is great! In order to keep your house and your guests neat, make sure the food is not too messy.

Make your main course ahead of time so you can enjoy the party.
If you're having a dinner party or a buffet, make lasagna or get a spiral ham so you don't have to be in the kitchen for most of the party. If you plan ahead, you can spend time with your guests while the food takes care of itself.

Set up separate beverage and food areas.
If you want guests to mingle awhile before dinner, set up two separate areas for drinks and appetizers, so that people aren't tripping over each other.

Set up a dessert station.
Keep desserts, dessert plates, and coffee cups and saucers near the coffee maker. It is vital that your kitchen is organized into sections when hosting a dinner party, and this will help remind you to turn on the coffee maker when you are preparing to serve dessert!

Prepare drink garnishes ahead of time.
Cut up all the citrus—lemons, limes, and oranges—and fill bowls with
olives and cherries. You can do this the night before, cover the bowls with
plastic wrap, and stick them in the fridge.

Put charms on wine glasses so they don't get mixed up.

Wine charms are a great invention! Slip a charm around each wine glass so that guests remember which one is theirs, and unwanted germs don't get spread around the party.

Set a small jar of toothpicks on the buffet table.

I know that I'm not the only person who hates to admit there is food stuck between my teeth! Put out a small jar or glass of toothpicks so guests don't have to ask for one.

Put small salt and pepper shakers on the table.

Put away the massive pepper grinder and put some dainty shakers on the table. This makes for a much more elegant touch.

Use place cards so guests aren't fumbling around at dinnertime.

You can get crafty and rubber-stamp your place cards, or you can simply write the guest's name. If guests know where to sit, they won't all be looking at you for direction. The last thing you need to do is play musical chairs while balancing dishes of hot food!

Always have an ample supply of napkins on hand.

Make sure there are cocktail and dinner napkins near food and on tables throughout the house. You never know when something might spill, and your guests will feel uncomfortable bringing a minor accident to your attention.

Make sure the dishwasher is empty prior to the party.

An empty dishwasher makes post-party cleanup that much quicker and easier. This is my husband's idea, since he's the one who ends up doing the dishes most of the time!

Have a suitable place for guests to put their coats and purses.

If you don't have a coat closet or rack in your entryway, plan to store coats in a bedroom or home office so that they're out of sight and out of the way.

Clean the areas of the house that guests will use most.

If you don't have time to clean every room in the house, focus on those that guests will see. Make sure that the kitchen, living room, and bathrooms are clean. If you're hanging coats in a closet, tidy it up first. Do the same for a bedroom if you plan to store coats in it.

Close the doors to any rooms you don't want guests going into.

Most people won't enter a room when the door is closed, unless you instruct them to do so. Plus, you can hide a mess if need be!

Make sure there are signs pointing guests to the function room.
If you're hosting a party somewhere other than your home, don't forget to show guests where to go. You don't want them wandering the halls of the function facility looking for the right room. You want your guests to be punctual, especially if it's a business party, and you can help them be on time by pointing them in the right direction.

CH

14

PARTIES:
THEIRS

Although you won't get axed for making a *faux pas* at your child's party, you will be left with a guilt you can't imagine. All it takes is just one teary-eyed puppy dog look from that sweet face, and you'll spend the next three birthdays trying to make up for the one that went awry! These tried-and-true tips will ensure dry eyes and big smiles.

Use a notebook to keep track of details.

I start planning birthday parties about two months ahead of time. In a spiral-bound notebook, write down the dates and times of the parties, a guest list, menu, party favors, and activities. It's a great way to remember everything that's important to your child in that particular year. Or if you're a spreadsheet person, get one going and put each year's details on a different tab.

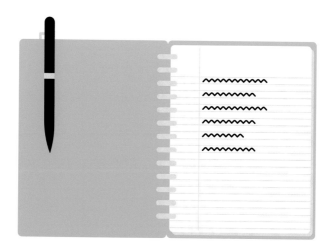

Jot down ideas as they come to you.

Throughout the party planning process, I constantly make changes to just about everything! I re-think the favors, the activities, and the decorations. It's hard to come up with fresh ideas year after year, but try to keep an open mind and let the brainstorming begin!

Do a "friend party" and a "family party" to separate age groups.

I always dreamed of just one birthday party for my daughter, but it never seemed to work out. We have a huge family, and they didn't have much in common with my daughter's friends. I never wanted my daughter to ignore her cousins because her friends were there (or vice versa), so I found it best to hold two parties. It's important to pay attention to the party guests so they know you appreciate their presence.

Establish an end time to the party.

Don't leave an invitation open-ended unless you want your child's guests to hang out afterwards. Also keep in mind that the birthday boy or girl might be tired after the party, and will need a good night's sleep.

Ask people to RSVP two weeks ahead of time.

Request a reply two weeks before the party, so you have time for last-minute snags. We once had a couple of last-minute replies, and I was scrambling to find the same party favors I had gotten for the other guests. Luckily, everything worked out and the party favors were a hit!

Include an email address so guests don't have to call to RSVP.

As said in the previous chapter, email is the ideal way for guests to RSVP. Given a choice, most people will respond via email, because it's fast and convenient. If you make it easy, you'll probably get a better response rate.

Plan a kid-friendly menu.

Make it easy! Kids don't care whether they have grilled filet mignon or a slice of pizza. If you're going to do lunch or dinner, choose a meal that can be prepared ahead of time, such as lasagna, or something that cooks quickly, such as hotdogs and hamburgers on the grill. If you want more time for party activities, opt for cake and ice cream, and skip the meal altogether. Just make sure that the time of the party is before or after mealtime, and you specify cake and ice cream on the party invitations, so guests know to eat beforehand.

Ask parents about food allergies.

While some kids may be aware of food allergies and vocal about asking what is in a certain food, others may not. So it's always a good idea to check with parents to see if their child has any dietary restrictions you should know about.

Make a shopping list and cross off items as you buy them.

Organize your shopping trip so that you don't waste a lot of time driving back and forth, and cross off items you no longer need to feel like you are making progress!

Put party favors in decorative bags so they're ready to go.

Whatever you do, make sure everyone receives the same party favor! Party favors shouldn't be expensive gifts, just little tokens to thank guests for coming. If you put the favors into small gift bags, you can easily hand them out at the end of the party. And if you give everyone the same favors, you don't need to bother writing names on the bags.

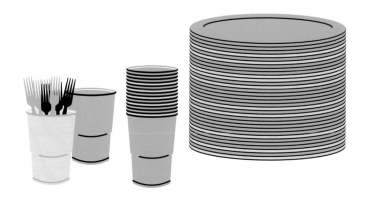

Lay out all serving dishes the night before the party.

The more you can get ready the night before, the easier your party day will be! If you don't have small animals that will climb onto the table, set out all the serving pieces. Then you can just fill them before the party starts.

Fill serving bowls with chips and snacks and cover them with plastic wrap.

Snacks such as chips and pretzels will stay fresh in serving bowls as long as you cover them tightly with plastic wrap. Do this the night before to save yourself time on party day.

Use paper plates and cups to make post-party pickup easier.
Instead of spending two hours doing dishes, use some cute paper plates and cups that can be discarded after the party. You can then spend those two hours with your feet up!

Lay out serving utensils the night before the party.
Put serving utensils, such as ladles and slotted spoons, next to the appropriate serving dish to make last minute preparations run smoothly.

Keep plastic utensils wrapped inside a napkin.
Use plastic utensils (color-coded to match the plates, cups, and napkins, of course!) so you can simply toss them after the party. Wrap a fork, knife, and spoon in one party napkin so they stay clean and people aren't scrambling for different utensils when it is time to eat.

Put wrapped utensils in a party cup.
Wrapped utensils will come unrolled unless you store them together. Put all of the utensil bundles into a party cup so they are easy for guests to grab.

Set up a beverage area and a food area.

Create separate areas for children to congregate. This will help deter a chaotic situation in your home.

Keep beverages in pitchers or in a cooler outside.

If your child's guests are old enough, let them serve themselves. Just make it easy for them to do by keeping chilled beverages, such as iced tea and lemonade, in pitchers, and soda cans and juice boxes in a cooler outside.

Freeze lemon wedges in ice cubes.

If you use pitchers, you need a way to keep those beverages cool and refreshing without being watered down. Freeze lemon wedges with a little water in an ice-cube tray, and place them in your lemonade or iced tea.

Order balloons so they're ready to be picked up on party day.

I used to waste time standing in line at the local party store for balloons on party day. But a two-minute phone call to your party store will save you an hour of waiting in line and give you time to attend to other last-minute details!

Ask your party store to group balloons into bunches.

Once you have the balloons, it can be a nightmare to untangle them and separate them into bunches. Ask the party store to tie balloons of various colors in bunches of three or four. Then put them by your mailbox, the deck, and around the table. Just be sure to keep the balloon bunches away from each other in the car on the way home!

Help guests find their way to the party.

If people have never been to your house before, tie a bunch of balloons to your street sign or mailbox, or have your child make a sign so that everyone knows where to go.

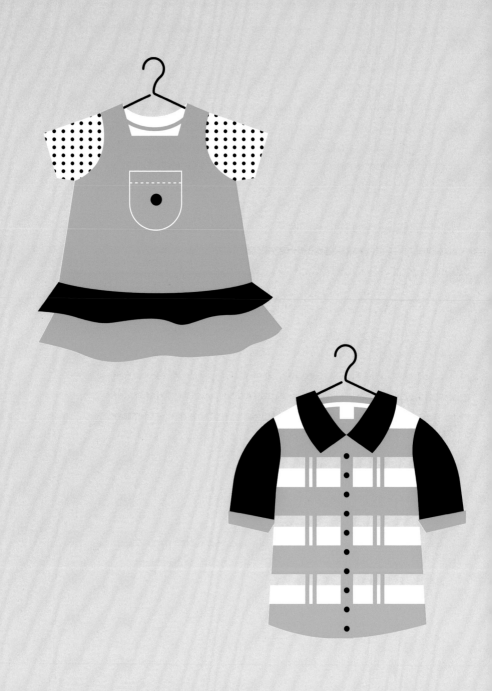

Prepare games and activities.
It's no secret that kids like to be entertained. Make sure your child's birthday party is one to remember by scheduling fun activities. You can do something elaborate such as rent a bounce house, or you can plan some simple games such as Pin the Tail on the Donkey, and relay races. Give out prizes to add to the excitement.

If you don't have time to put party favors together, buy a piñata.
Kids love tackling a piñata to get out their goodies! Fill it with age-appropriate candy and trinkets, and hand out party bags to make collecting the candy a little easier.

If you don't have a lot of inside space, rent a tent.
Rain dates are especially hard to schedule when it comes to kids. If the party is rained out, your child will be really disappointed, and all of your hard work will go right out the window. If there is bad weather in the forecast, rent a tent. You certainly don't want to plan a party twice!

Get the party girl or boy's outfit ready the night before.
This is a good idea, especially if you need to iron the outfit. Make sure it is clean and ready to party!

Bake the cake or cupcakes the day before the party.
This way, the cupcakes will be fresh, but you'll also have time to correct any mistakes! Once the baking is done, you can focus on the all-important cake decorating.

Clean your house before the party.

A week before the party, plan to do a little bit of cleaning each day, so you can squeeze in other party preparations, such as cooking and baking, as well. For example, dust on Wednesday, clean the kitchen on Thursday, and clean the bathrooms the day before the party. You want your bathrooms to be squeaky clean for your guests!

Plan meals for out-of-town guests.

If you have out-of-town guests staying with you, make something you can prepare ahead of time, or simply plan to go out.

Decorate the house the night before the party.

With the exception of latex balloons, all party decorations can be hung the night before the party. That way, you have time to change your mind about placement!

Set the timer on the coffee maker so fresh coffee is ready for the adults.

Kids' parties fly by for the kids, but don't forget the adults might need a little pick-me-up to make it through.

Keep track of presents.

Set out a pen and a sheet of paper near the gifts so you can write down what your child receives and from whom. You'll have an easier time writing thank you notes, and you won't need to rummage through the trash to find a gift card that was thrown out by accident.

Buy thank-you notes ahead of time.

It's always a good idea to keep note cards on hand. Encourage your children to help you write thank-you notes, so they develop good manners early on. If your child isn't old enough to write the notes, have her sign her name or draw a picture.

Keep a list of names and addresses of party guests.

Keep a list of invited guests and their addresses so you can quickly and correctly address the thank-you notes. You may want to hang on to that list for next year's party, too!

PART
THREE

On the Move

15

VACATIONS AND
BUSINESS TRIPS

You don't want to spend a week on the road only to find out that your destination is closed, so be sure to plan ahead. Strong organization will make for a trouble-free trip.

Set up a notebook or download an app to organize all travel details. This is especially important if you're going on an extended vacation or to several different places. Keep track of transportation details, whether it's via airplane, bus, or ship, as well as hotel accommodations and any special tours you're scheduling. Be sure to include contact names and phone numbers in case you get stuck someplace! There are also several apps that help keep your trip on track by allowing you to connect with other travelers, receive updates on flights, and make reservations.

Make notes of all appointments before you go.

If you're traveling for business, take down all of your appointments in your planner or on your phone before you leave. It's easy to get sidetracked when you're in a new place.

Keep a list of all business contact information.

Make sure you know where you're going! Include meeting locations and the names of the individuals you're meeting with. It's a good idea to map out directions before the day of your meeting so you're not late.

Keep track of mileage.

Even if you're not a salesman, you'll find that most companies pay for mileage that is directly related to business. Keep track of this so you can be reimbursed for expenses.

Buy a hands-free device for your cell phone.

It may not be a law in your state now, but it probably will be shortly. Regardless of how well you drive, you do become distracted when you try to do two things at once. It's very hard to hold a cell phone and safely maneuver a car at the same time. Keep your hands on the wheel!

Ask AAA to map out your road trip.

If you're an AAA member, ask them to map out your route. The maps are highlighted with the quickest route, and they include everything from where to stop and eat to which roads are under construction.

Book the hotel early.

Hotels always offer great deals, but you may be eligible for an even better rate. If you're an AAA member or an AARP member, be sure to check if you can get a discount.

Notify the hotel of any special requirements.

Give your hotel advance notice of any special accommodations you'll need during your stay. The earlier you book, the better your chances of getting what you need, such as a non-smoking room, an extra bed, or a crib.

Make a note of check-in and checkout times so you can plan accordingly.

In my opinion, check-in and checkout times should be reversed! I would much rather check in at noon and check out at 3:00 P.M. Call your hotel or visit their website to find out when you should arrive and when you should schedule your departure.

Find out what restaurants and attractions are in the vicinity.

If you're not traveling with a tour group, make note of nearby restaurants and attractions ahead of time. Check out apps such as Yelp and TripAdvisor for recommendations, or do a quick web search for must-see sights at your destination. Make the most of your time while you're there!

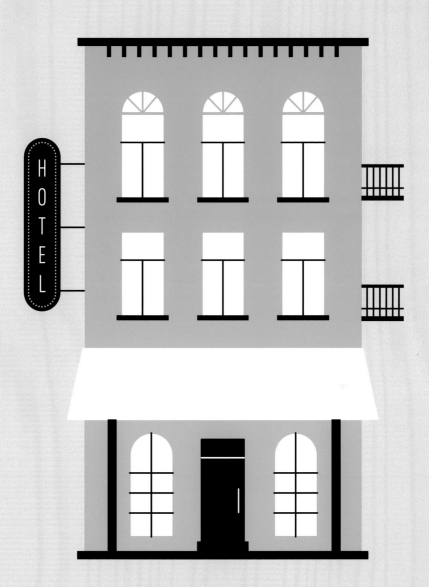

Create a day-by-day excursion planner.

Once you know what is in and around the area you'll be staying in, make a list of what want to see, and then make a tentative schedule of activities. Remember, you may need to adjust the schedule due to bad weather, so plan some optional indoor activities to be safe. If you plan carefully beforehand, you won't miss out on something you or a family member really wants to do or see. It's easy to forget things in the excitement of traveling!

Make trip planning a family affair.

My dad always made sure that each of us had some input in our family vacations, whether it was choosing a restaurant or a destination. I remember our two-week trip to Hawaii when I was sixteen years old. Dad let my younger sister pick one island and let me pick the other. Encouraging kids to take part in the planning makes vacations special for everyone.

If flying, keep an eye on prices.

Experts recommended you book flights anywhere from 6 months to 2 weeks before your trip, which seems like a pretty large window of time. However, downloading certain apps or setting up a price alert make it easier to monitor the fluctuating prices of airfare and tell you when it is the ideal time to book your specific flight.

Review your airline tickets and check in online if possible.

E-tickets may be the best way to go as far as time is concerned, but I always like to have my ticket in hand. If you find any errors, report them immediately so that you don't have any surprises at the gate! If you don't need to check bags, online check-in allows you to get your boarding pass ahead of time and go right to security, avoiding lines at the check-in desks.

Pack snacks for the plane ride.

You can't predict a late incoming flight or engine failure, so be prepared. Pack a few snacks in your carry-on bag, just in case!

Send your itinerary to a close family member or friend.

It is important that someone knows where you are and how to reach you throughout your trip.

Make a list of items to be packed for each family member.

If you make a list of what to pack, older kids can pack for themselves. By involving them in the preparations, they'll be more excited about the trip.

Roll your clothes to save space.

Do you have any idea how many rolled shirts you can cram into your suitcase? Neither do I, but it's a lot! Not only will you save space, your clothes will be less wrinkled when you arrive.

Don't over-pack.

I never take my own advice! I always set out with the best of intentions, but end up bringing home a bag of clean clothes that were never worn. You don't want your bag to be too heavy to maneuver, and you don't want to end up carrying bags that are too heavy for other family members to carry. Everyone should be able to carry his or her own luggage, so plan accordingly.

Don't pack a lot of jewelry.

Choose simple accessories that can be worn every day. For example, wear a simple pair of stud earrings that you don't have to remove at night and that you can wear with everything.

Bring plastic bags to store wet clothing and bathing suits.

If you're like my family and plan on getting in one last swim before you check out of the hotel, pack some plastic bags so you can protect the other clothes in your suitcase.

Deflate your beach balls so you have room for more gear.

Going to the beach? Keep in mind that inflatable beach toys can be deflated for travel. Just don't forget to pack that air pump!

Pack clothes that can be mixed and matched.

If you don't have a set of ten suitcases and someone to carry them for you, pack light! A great way to save space is to pack outfits that can be interchanged—for example, skirts and pants of the same solid color, so you can wear the same tops with them.

Pack a full-sized bar of soap.

Have you ever been stranded in the shower with a bar of soap that's one-inch square? I have one too many times! Not only does a full bar of soap last longer, but it is more efficient. Cleaning your 2,000 body parts with a flake of soap that slips out of your hand every two seconds can take hours, so be sure to bring a bar from home.

Pack sunglasses, sunscreen, and hats.

Depending on where you're going, you may need protection from the sun. Some areas, especially those near the equator, can get extremely hot with the sun's intensive rays. You don't want to spend your vacation recovering from heat stroke or third-degree burns in a hotel room or a foreign hospital, so cover up!

Bring dish detergent to wash children's cups and bottles.
Instead of packing a cup or bottle for each feeding, pack a small bottle of dish detergent and some wipes. You can wash the cups at the end of each day and use them again the following day.

Don't pack anything that will slow you down at the airport.
Getting through the airport may take some time, so think before you pack. Don't pack anything that will be cause for alarm, such as knives, scissors, or razor blades. If you need any of these items, just buy them when you get to your destination. It's also a good idea to pack your TSA-approved liquids in a plastic bag before you get to the airport, and store it in a place that is easy to access when it is time to take them out.

Be prepared for security.
Undressing and redressing at security can take up a lot of time—more so if you're running late for a flight. Avoid getting slowed down by wearing slip-on shoes with socks. This way, you can easily remove your shoes for security and not have to walk in the airport barefoot. Another tip is to wear elastic pants instead of a belt, which you'll likely be required to remove.

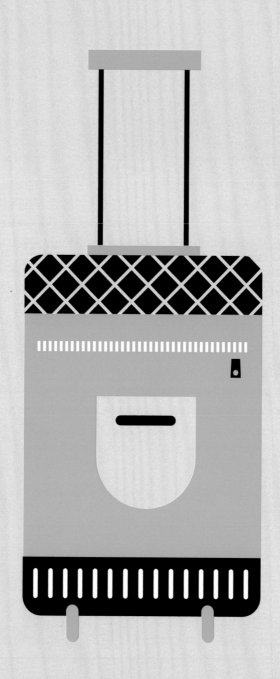

Pack your carry-on as if it were your only bag.

Organize all contact information, airline boarding passes, and passports in your carry-on bag. In fact, make sure that *everything* related to your transportation and hotel accommodations is in your carry-on bag and easily accessible. In the event that your luggage is lost, you'll still be able to proceed with your trip.

Keep necessities in your carry-on.

Airlines lose luggage all the time, so make sure you have a change of clothes, deodorant, and toothbrush with you in your carry-on bag. If there is something that you cannot live without for a day, such as a medication, make sure it's in there, too.

Pack activities for the kids in your carry-on.

Trust me, you'll need something to entertain your children even if you expect to have a short flight! Pack a few small books, coloring books, crayons, and a small toy. If you allow your kids screen time, load up your tablet or smartphone with all of their favorite videos ahead of your trip.

Pack valuables in your carry-on.

If you do decide to bring expensive jewelry with you, pack it in your carry-on so that it stays with you at all times.

Buy travel-sized shampoo, conditioner, deodorant, and toothpaste.
Instead of packing all of your full-sized toiletries from home, buy the travel-sized versions to save space and to make sure you can get them through security if you put them in your carry-on bag.

Keep travel wipes in your purse.
I always keep wipes in my purse for dirty faces, hands, tables, chairs, and anything else that needs a good cleaning. You don't need to pack a tub of baby wipes, just a slim travel pack.

Make sure your bags have luggage tags with contact information.
Even if you have a bright red suitcase and you know there isn't another one like it, put a tag on it. Include your name, address, and telephone number so the airline can reach you if your bag gets lost.

Pack gum for chewing while taking off and landing.
An old friend of mine will not fly, because he hates that popping in his ears. He's right, it hurts! Even if you're a frequent flyer, chewing gum when taking off and landing can ease the pressure. You don't want your kids to have a painful flight and an unpleasant memory!

Keep a first-aid kit in your bag.
You never know when a jellyfish will sting you, or your daughter will step on a crab, so be prepared!

Unpack as soon as you arrive.
Unpack when you arrive to let the wrinkles fall out of your clothes. Once you've emptied your suitcase, you can use it to store your dirty clothes so they're out of sight.

Store valuables in the hotel safe, and keep a list of what you put in there.
Most hotels offer storage for your valuables. If you're bringing expensive jewelry or important documents with you, store them in the hotel safe. Be sure to keep track of what you put in there so you can recover any losses if necessary.

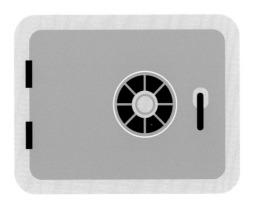

Arrange for someone to take care of your pets and water your plants.
If you don't like putting your pets in a kennel, ask a friend, neighbor, or pet sitter to care for them while you're gone. If you have numerous pets, or exotic plants, have them come to the house ahead of time, and walk them through exactly what they'll need to do. Leave a detailed set of instructions, put all supplies in an obvious place, prominently post your contact information and your vet's phone number, and make sure you get the sitter a little something to say thank you! If you're leaving for an extended period of time, hire a professional pet sitter and ask someone else to water your plants.

Ask a neighbor to keep an eye on your house.
If you don't have someone coming to take care of pets or water plants, ask a neighbor to keep an eye on things for you. Tell them when you're leaving and when you're returning, so that they can keep lookout for anything suspicious. Also, make sure your neighbor has your contact information!

Hire someone to mow the lawn.
If you're going to be gone for a couple of weeks (or more—lucky you!), make sure you arrange for someone to mow the lawn. An overgrown lawn is a dead giveaway that nobody's home! Same goes for shoveling if you're traveling in the winter.

Let your bank know you are traveling.

It is common for banks to assume that charges are fraudulent if they come from a faraway location. While the extra security is comforting, having your account frozen while traveling is extremely inconvenient. Before you leave, call your bank or go to their website to let them know when and where you are traveling so you'll always have access to your funds.

Make sure you can use your phone.

If you're traveling internationally, chances are your cell phone will not work once you cross the border. Check with your cell phone carrier about temporary international plans or getting a new SIM card in the country you are visiting. Another option is to use free WiFi calling/messaging apps on your smartphone.

Call your doctor to see if you need any vaccinations.

If you're traveling abroad, make sure that your vaccinations are up to date and that you have the appropriate immunizations for the country you're visiting. Also check the CDC website for recommended vaccines and make an appointment with your doctor well in advance of your departure date.

Tell the post office to suspend your mail.

A week or so before you leave, go to the post office website and arrange for them to hold your mail. This way, your mailbox won't overflow, and it won't be so obvious that you are out of town. The same goes for any newspaper or subscription mail service you may regularly receive.

Ask your children's teachers to assign homework so they don't fall behind.

My parents always asked us to get homework from our teachers before going on vacation. What a drag! But seriously, if your kids are going to miss more than a few days of school, talk to their teachers to see what they can do while they're away. I'm sure they'd rather spend a little time studying than stay back a year!

If taking a road trip, map out interesting sites to stop at en route.
Get the whole family involved in road trip planning by asking children
to pick out destinations along the route. If you make frequent trips to a
certain place—to see family, for example—take a different route each time
to keep the trip exciting and different.

Keep an atlas in your car, even if you have GPS.
It is wise to keep a road atlas and other maps in your car in case you wind
up in an area that has spotty cell phone service or your navigation system
dies. When I got my first car, my dad gave me a map of what looked like
the world. I didn't understand why I needed a map of Maryland when I
lived in Connecticut, but wouldn't you know I got lost in Maryland the
following year! When I called my dad in tears, he told me to look at the
map he had put in my backseat.

Make a playlist that is a mix of everyone's music.
My mother had a saying when we were growing up, and it was "my car, my
radio." Needless to say, we didn't have much choice but to hit and pinch
each other in the backseat while listening to elevator music. As a parent, I
would much rather listen to toddler favorites for an hour than have a fight.
A playlist is an easy way to make sure everyone hears a song or two they
like. You could also have each family member make their own playlist and
take turns listening to each one.

Have each child pack a small "entertainment" tote.
You can only sing bus songs for so long! Ask your children to put together
a few of their favorite books, games, and activities, so they can keep
themselves occupied on a road trip.

Fill covered plastic cups with snacks.

We always knew we were headed somewhere when we saw the tall Tupperware cups come out of the cabinet! My mother packed a cup of Cheerios for each of us so we wouldn't have to stop as often. As long as you pack some family favorites, it's a great way to ward off crankiness and hunger pains. Otherwise, buy juice and snacks once you get to your destination.

If road-tripping with your pet, keep water, food, and a leash easily accessible.

Make sure that your pet has an adequate food and water supply for the trip. Stop every once in a while to let your pet run around and go to the bathroom. (Don't forget to pack clean-up bags.) The stops will be a good time for everyone to stretch their legs.

CH

16

MAKING YOUR MOVE

Moving can be a nightmare, but it doesn't have to be. The hardest move for me was across the hall to a bigger apartment, and the easiest move was to a house three hours away. The time, distance, and size of the move are irrelevant when it comes to organization—the details are vital! Here are some ways to make moving relatively painless.

Make a to-do list and keep it updated.

Whether you're moving across the street or across the country, there are a million things to do. Keep a list of what needs to be done and when. If you make the list on your phone or computer, you can organize it chronologically, and then make updates as needed.

Obtain several estimates from moving companies and check references.

Moving costs can vary significantly, and you want to make sure you get the most for your money. I cannot say it enough: Check references! Our old neighbors used a moving company that destroyed their furniture, stole their cutlery, and took roughly fourteen hours (billing by the hour, of course) to move them down the street. Don't let this happen to you. Ask movers to provide you with three references or check with the Better Business Bureau.

Tell movers of any items that require additional insurance coverage.
Moving companies will sell you additional coverage for items that are
not covered by the standard insurance. But before you buy additional
coverage, review your current homeowner's policy to find out if the
items are already covered.

Write down all the details.
Write down the number of movers hired, their hourly rate, and who at
the moving company authorized the contract. You should not only receive
a hard copy of the contract but you should also keep your own notes.
Record the names of the people you spoke with, the date, and what they
told you. Even if you've gotten positive feedback from the references the
company provided you with, you never know what they may try to get
away with.

Take measurements in your new home for rugs, curtains, and so on.
If you know what you'll need before you move in, you can set up your new
house in no time!

Get rid of anything you no longer use.
If you don't use it, lose it before the move. There is no sense in packing
things that you'll never use in your new home. Have a yard sale, sell stuff
on online, give things to friends and family (if you know they'd like them),
and take the rest to the thrift store or consignment shop.

Send a change of address message to friends and family.
Email friends and family that you will be moving, and be sure to include the date you'll be at your new address.

Notify your post office, creditors, and utility companies of your new address.
If you rely on the mail to tell you when your bills are due, make sure you give advance notice of your move to the postmaster and any creditors.

Notify magazine and catalog companies of your new address.
It's not only important that you get your mail at your new address, but also that the people living in your old home don't get bombarded with loads of junk mail and magazines intended for you.

Call doctors, dentists, and schools and request that your records be transferred.
When you decide to move, some of the first things you should do are find a new doctor, dentist, and school. Once you've confirmed that they're accepting new patients and students, transfer your records and school transcripts so they'll be waiting for you when you arrive.

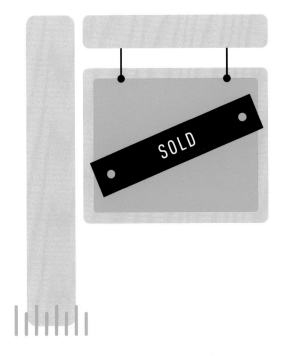

Clean your new place before filling it up.

I am a cleaning fanatic, and I will not move into a home until I've thoroughly cleaned it. If you can clean your house the day before, the move will go smoothly. If you can't get in early, pack all of your cleaning supplies into a crate and keep them in your car so they don't accidentally end up on the moving truck.

Buy moving boxes and packing tape.

Do you have any idea how much money you'll save if you pack your own house? Most movers charge by the hour, so save some money and get packing!

Use everyday fabric items and old newspapers to wrap dishes and other breakables.

There is no need to buy packing paper from a moving company when you have wrapping materials at home. In addition to old newspapers or weekly ads you get in the mail, use the towels, cloth napkins, placemats, and tablecloths you need to pack anyway as wrapping for fragile items. You'll cut down on waste and make fewer trips to the moving truck as a result.

Pack one room at a time and stack boxes.

Packing an entire room might take you more than ten minutes, depending on the size, but start with a corner of the room and take it ten minutes at a time. The more organized you are in packing, the more organized you'll be on moving day.

Label each box on the top and sides.

Buy a giant black marker and label your boxes so that there is no confusion as to what is inside or where they should go.

Stack packed boxes by the door.

After you pack all the rooms, stack the moving boxes near the front door. Remember, movers charge by the hour, so make their job faster.

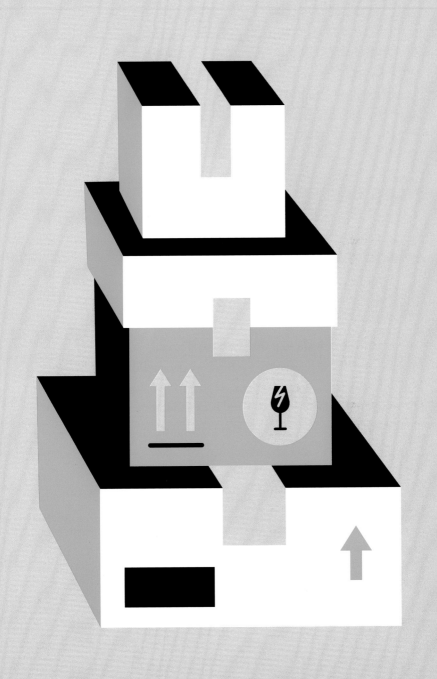

Encourage your kids to pack their own toys.

My daughter was 2½ years old when we moved, and she had a blast playing in the toy box putting away all of her toys! It made her feel grown-up to help with the move, and it gave me some time to concentrate on other things.

Pack essentials in their own box.

Use one box for paper cups and plates, plastic utensils, napkins, paper towels, soap, and toilet paper. And if you think you might treat helpers to a pizza dinner, pack extras! Put this box in your car so it is easily accessible on moving day.

Store extra appliances.

Put all kitchen appliances and gadgets you don't use in a separate box labeled "Storage". This is especially important when you're downsizing to a smaller home. Pack these appliances away and make do. Or, it might be time to sell them or make a donation to Goodwill!

Put valuables in your car.

It's a good idea to transport your own jewelry and anything else you wouldn't want lost in a move. Even if you've checked references and deemed the moving company to be reputable, you never know what goes on once the trucks are on the road. Make sure your valuables are safely packed, and in your locked car before the movers arrive.

Make sure your furniture is wrapped prior to going on the truck.

Before anything gets moved, it should be adequately protected. Ask that this be specified in the contract. The move will be half over by the time your $30,000 bedroom set is on the truck!

Ask a friend or relative to watch small children and pets during the move.

Your doors will be open throughout the move, and it is very easy for a pet to escape. If there isn't anyone who can take your pets for the day, lock them inside the bathroom with food, water, and a favorite toy. Make sure young children are either out of the house with a babysitter or watched closely during the move. The movers, not to mention the parents, don't want children underfoot.

Make a mental note of the mover's start and finish times.

Don't forget, movers charge by the hour! Remember my friends who moved down the street in fourteen hours? The movers spent half the time chatting inside the truck! Don't get raked over the coals when it comes time to pay the bill. Know what you were promised and what actually took place. If there is any discrepancy, ask to speak to a manager before you complete the transaction.

Have one person at the new house to direct the movers.

You don't want to show up to find your bedroom set in the living room and your kitchen table in the basement! Have someone there who is familiar with the layout of the house and knows where all the items go.

Inspect all your furniture before the movers leave.

Before you sign on the dotted line, make sure your belongings are in the same condition as when you packed them.

Ask for help with unpacking.

Allow friends and relatives to help you unpack, even if they put things in
the wrong place! Try not to sweat the small stuff, and just be thankful that
you have help. You can always move things around once you're in.

Organize lunch for your moving buddies.

If you're moving locally, thank your friends for their efforts by treating
them to pizza and beer on the floor of your new house.

Make the beds as soon as they're set up.

Moving is tiring, and when your day is done, you just want to collapse
into a nice, clean bed—not dig out the clean sheets and make every
bed in the house! To avoid this, make up all your beds as soon as they're
put together.

Unpack your kids' rooms first.

Moving is a huge adjustment for everyone, especially children. It's hard
to get used to a new house, new school, and new friends. There isn't much
you can do about school and friends, but you can certainly make their new
house comfortable and familiar so they feel at home right away.

Have a special gift waiting at the new house for each child.
It might help your kids to adjust to their new surroundings if something special is waiting for them at the new house. For example, I set up a Strawberry Shortcake tent in my daughter's new room the night before we moved in. She loved the surprise, and moving into the new house became a fun adventure.

Arrange for old friends to come and visit soon after you move in.
Ease the trauma of moving by welcoming friends and family to your new home. This can even be arranged before you move, so that you and your kids have something to look forward to.

About the Author

S ara Hunter is a mother and holds down a marketing
job while keeping her house spotlessly clean and
organized. She lives in North Attleboro, Massachusetts.

INDEX

B

Bathroom
bar soaps, 40
bath toys, 43
cleaning supplies, 42
cosmetics, 34–35
cotton swabs, squares, and balls, 37
extra supplies, 42
frequently used items, 41
hair styling tools, 35
magazines and books, 41
medications, 36–37
nail polish, 35
razors, 42
seasonal items, 40
toiletries, 34
toothbrushes, 41
towels, 39, 40
tweezers and scissors, 37

Bedroom, master
baseball caps, 63
clothes no longer wearing, 62
dirty clothes, 59
hand cream and lip balm, 60
hanging clothes, 62–63
magazines and books, 60
out-of-season clothes, 59
robes, 60
running pants and sweatpants, 59
shoes, 63
shorts, 59
socks, lingerie, and pantyhose, 58
T-shirts, 59
tie rack, 63

Bedrooms, children's
baby books, 73
beach accessories, 74
books, 69
children's artwork and letters, 73
chores calendar, 75
clothing to grow into, 70
dance items, 74
dirty clothes, 71
hair accessories, 66
hats and caps, 67
jewelry, 67
keepsakes, 69
Kinderprint ID card, 73
outgrown and out-of-season clothes, 70
pajamas, 70
photos, 72
purses and backpacks, 67
school items, 74
shoes, 67
stuffed animals, 69
toys and balls, 69
underwear, tights, and socks, 70
vacation pictures, 72

G

Garage
auto supplies, 114
bicycles, 113
fasteners, 115
gardening tools and supplies, 112, 114
outdoor toys, 113
shoe mat, 115
sleds, 113
snow tires, 113
strollers, 113
umbrellas, 115

H

Holiday entertaining
greeting card list, 120
party gifts, 131
party to-dos ahead of time, 120–125, 132
party to-dos day of party, 125–126, 128, 129, 132–133
party to-dos night before, 126, 128

Home office
bank information, 89
bill paying, 89
budget preparation, 90
bulletin or white boards, 93
business cards, 87
calendars, using, 78, 79, 95
clipboards, 83
computer, 84–87
credit cards, 90–91
customer files, 92–93
desk organization, 80
documents, 84
employee reminders, 94–95
file cabinets, 84
folders, 84
greeting cards, 79
low-inventory items list, 83
meeting notes, 95
paper, 83
paperclips, 82
payroll preparation, 94
pens, pencils, scissors, 82–83
phone, 87, 89, 92
safes, 79
user manuals and warranty information, 79

Houseguests
arrival and departure times, 140
bathroom for, 140
food for, 136–137, 139, 140, 141
preparing guestroom, 136, 137
spending time with, 141

K

Kitchen
appliances, 23
artwork on fridge, 31
baking pans, 22
canned goods, 21
cereal, 21
cleaners, 28
cookbooks, 18
cooking utensils, 16
coupons, 29

cups, 24
dishes, 24
dishtowels, 28
flatware and utensils, 16
food in fridge and freezer, 26
food wrap, 25
fruit, 19
glasses, 24
juice boxes, 26
lids, 17
mail and bills, 29
mugs, 22
pans, 17, 22
pens and paper, 29
plates, 24
potholders, 28
pots, 17, 22
recipes, 18–19
reusable water bottles, 25
seasoning packets, 19
shopping lists, 30
snacks, 21
spice jars, 19
sponges, 28
stainless steel bowls and
  covers, 16
storage containers and
  bags, 25
take-out menus, 31
tea bags, 22

L
Laundry room
  drying rack, 98
  laundering supplies, 98,
  100, 101
  laundry bag or hamper, 98
  mending/ironing piles, 100
  plastic hangers, 100
Living room
  candles and holders, 48
  CDs, 47
  coats and jackets, 48
  DVDs, 47
  family pictures, 49
  home videos, 46
  letter rack/key hook, 49
  magazines, 47
  toys, 49

M
Moving
  food and, 204
  moving companies, 194–195,
  203
  new home preparations,
  195, 197
  notifications of new address,
  196
  packing for, 198, 200, 201
  records to be transferred, 196
  small children and pets and,
  203, 205
  to-do list, 194
  unpacking, 204
  valuables, 201
Mudroom
  winter gear, 74

P
Parties
  delegating responsibilities,
  145
  food, 145, 147, 149
  organizing house for,
  152–153
  planning information, 144
  setting table, 151
  timeline, 145
Parties, children's
  balloons, 162–163
  beverages, 162
  day/night before to-dos,
  160, 165
  end time, 157
  favors, 158, 165
  food, 158, 162, 165
  for friends and family, 157
  games and activities, 165
  organizing house for, 166
  planning information, 156
  plates, cups, and utensils, 161
  presents and thank-you
  notes, 167
  RSVPs, 157
Playroom
  art supplies, 52
  board games, 55
  building blocks, 54

doll clothes, 55
dolls, 52
plastic totes for, 53
play food, 55
playhouse dishes and
  utensils, 55
small toys, 52, 54
trains and track
  accessories, 53

S
Storage solutions
  cake decorating supplies, 105
  craft supplies, 105
  gift wrapping supplies, 106
  ornaments, 106
  photo albums, 109
  scrapbook materials, 108

T
Travel
  care of home while away, 186
  carry-on bag, 183–185
  clothes, 178, 179–180
  flights, 176–177, 184
  health, 189
  homework assignments, 189
  at hotel, 185
  notifications, 188, 189
  organizing details, 172–174
  packing, 178–180, 183
  phone use, 188
  planning sites and activities,
  176
  road trip necessities, 190,
  191
  snacks, 191